Don't Believe Your Lying Eyes

N. L. Thomas, Ph.D.

G. T. Laird, MAT

N. Jennings

ISBN   978-0-578-73622-8

SJE Publishing Detroit, Michigan 313-757-6111

Printed by 48 Hr Books in the United States

CONTENT

FORWARD   1

AND HE PLAYED THE GAME WELL   2

FLAME THROWER   21

FLIP..THAT...NARC   38

FOR FUCK'S SAKE   56

SEX AS A WEAPON   75

CULT OF THE NORTH NARC   89

DIFFERENT STRAINS OF THE NARC VIRUS   107

AMANDA WALLER   125

I AIN'T TRYNA' FIX NOBODY   141

FULL ASSESSMENT   161

BIBLIOGRAPHY   181

ABOUT THE AUTHORS...   182

To: Mae

Thanks for your constant encouragement and support in everything I do. You have been a driving force in my confidence to succeed.
I really appreciate you.

FORWARD

Have you ever been in an intimate relationship or think you are in an intimate relationship with a person who has Narcissistic Personality Disorder (NPD)? Well, we have! After having several phone conversations with two of my friends and noting experiencing similar relationship woes, we decided to tell our story. Being in an intimate relationship with a narcissist, even for a short period of time, can cause long-lasting effects emotionally, psychologically, and financially. According to the Diagnostic and Statistical Manual of Mental Disorder (2013), NPD is a mental condition in which a person has an inflated sense of their own importance, a deep admiration of self, a great need for attention, experience problematic relationships with friends and partners, as well as lack empathy for others. Yet, these behaviors hide their fragile ego, lack of confidence, and low self-esteem that are highly sensitive to criticism. Discover three friends' journey of self-doubt, self-discovery, and self-healing.

We hope this book will provide tools to those in a relationship with a narcissistic person to exit the relationship and help rebuild their self-esteem. This book can also be used as a learning instrument for mental health professionals to address the emotional distress of clients after being in a toxic relationship with a narcissist.

~N. L. Thomas

1

AND HE PLAYED THE GAME WELL

Phoenix: What up doe Ginger and Glynn!! How is everything going?

Ginger: Could be better, or worse, I suppose.

Glynn: Meh. [laughing nervously]

Phoenix: How's the baby, Glynn?

Glynn: Excellent question. I am currently being boxed out, so I don't know. His birthday is this weekend and I am getting misinformation regarding my role in his life. As it stands, it is unclear who is genuinely advocating for me to be a father, and who is only concerned with a more individualistic motive. It seems more like the information I receive is meant to keep my mental subroutines locked in a state of emotional processing, preventing the correct action allocation.

Phoenix: Your role?!!? Are you freakin' kidding me? That shit is unreal. So, she is still trying to control everything?

Ginger: She's not trying! She is doing it!

Glynn: At least that is her perception. There is a lot happening that is constantly affecting me. Reaching out to her is useless unless I grovel in some way she deems acceptable. It is a game I used to play, but I haven't the energy to engage in anymore. So, my punishment is no communication whatsoever regarding anything.

Ginger: So what are your next steps? Do you have a plan?

Glynn: No. As of now, my plan is to work on improving myself and my situation. It's the only thing I can do to keep from self-deprecating. I feel trapped in a well of anxiety. One of y'all got Lassie's number?

Phoenix: Boy you are insane! You know this is part of her plan to keep you confused and frustrated. Oh, the games that narcissists play. But I do like that you plan on working on yourself.

Ginger: They will dangle a whole human in your face to get what they want!

Phoenix: And tell you everything is your fault.

Glynn: That's very true! It feels very similar to hostage negotiation. Like, whenever I don't give in to her unreasonable demands, she blames me for the punishment she is inflicting.

Ginger: Gaslighting is one of their greatest tools!

Glynn: Yes! But it's the emotional gaslighting that has me the most perplexed, I'd say?

Ginger and Phoenix: All of it is emotional!

Glynn: If so, then that's what bothers me. I keep looking for the logic in her unethical, seemingly irrational actions. I'm just. . . I don't know. [holding and shaking his head]

Phoenix: Hey Glynn, any word from the DHS?

Glynn: No. But I have yet to reach out. I don't even know where to begin. There is so much that has occurred that I am unaware of how to provide a proper perspective on my situation. At best, it sounds like a jumbled mess of battered spouse stories from the Lifetime channel.

Phoenix: You had your first meeting already and they have not contacted you anymore? They may drop the case. [shoulder shrugs]

Glynn: Oh, you mean CPS? At least, I think it was CPS. At any rate, everything was dropped, yes.

Phoenix: [laughing] Yes, I meant CPS. Thank goodness! At least that is one less thing to worry about.

Ginger: It's like a Twilight Zone episode that keeps repeating!

Phoenix: I know! She keeps up a lot of confusion and plays mind games. Ginger, is mister man still "working" on remodeling your bathroom?

Ginger: Yes, at my mental expense!

Glynn: What about your financial expense?

Phoenix: He will make this a job that will take a year to finish.

Ginger: Yes he will! He's over every day, fixing one thing at a time; beating me down with love bombs, future fakes, unbelievable promises, then discards. Financially, he's not doing anything in that regard. He's picking up the tabs on some things that I need to finish but that's part of the Love Bombing.

Phoenix: He has to make himself look good for others. You know he is going to tell everyone he did it for free, out of the kindness of his heart. As if he was one.

Glynn: Yes! Appearances are extremely important to them, as they cannot be seen as lesser than. Any attempt to ground them in the reality of their situation results in a visceral defensive reaction.

Ginger: Very true, Glynn! He's very careful, doing everything perfectly.

Phoenix: So, my narc is being indicted for cross-state cocaine trafficking and facing 15 years in prison.

Glynn: Holy shit!

Ginger: Lucky you! I mean...What the hell? Wait! Wait! Wait! Phoenix, you have to start from the beginning! Do tell!

Phoenix: Well, you both know that I met Chris on an online dating site with a fish as a logo. I should have known something was fishy from the start. But, my co-worker and a few clients had met some good guys and two of my clients married the guys. So, I felt comfortable and hopeful that I would meet someone too.

Ginger: I heard those sites were narc hunting grounds! Keep going.

Phoenix: I wish someone would have told me that before I was psychologically ambushed. But anyway, we talked via the app for about two or three months before exchanging numbers. He was so charming over the phone. And fine! He was 6'4 with an athletic build. His jawline was chiseled like Robert Pattison from the Twilight movies. We talked about our goals, family values, and what we wanted in a mate. He said he wanted a long-lasting relationship that he and I could grow old together and sit on the front porch and tell our grandchildren how we met. He said, "I want a grandparent's love." He said all the right things. He told me he was originally from Jamaica. That his birth mother is in jail for killing her abusive boyfriend. He told me an American family adopted him but the father was physically abusive to him. According to Chris, his father would beat him for no reason. He called him slow and retarded because of his poor grades. He was in special education classes due to his language barrier. He said he had a heavy Jamaican accent and his teachers couldn't understand him. He also said he was in foster care for a while. His story made me feel bad for him and my empathy kicked in. We would talk on the phone for hours every night for about another two months before we actually met in person. He was unemployed but going to truck driving school to "change" his life. Oh, I forgot to mention that he had already served time for international drug trafficking. Silly me! Thinking he wanted to change and start a new life. I must be an empath or a special type of fool to have believed his bullshit.

Glynn: He did want a different life. But he didn't want a clean start.

Phoenix: Looking back at the situation, I think he wanted a clean life but he couldn't get out of the lifestyle. Things were good for a while and I met his family. As we got closer, I would hear little stories of his past lifestyle. How he ran drugs and would bring people from other countries into the United States. My antennas began to rise and I started listening more. But, I continued to stay with this man.

Glynn: Wait, there was human trafficking, too?

Phoenix: It sounds like it. He only mentioned it once but that part was never made clear. Anyway, he would go on road trips with me for my organization. I thought it was great to have him by my side, doing all the driving, carrying my bags, opening doors, and all the stuff a caring man should do for his lady. But, it appears he used me to help transport drugs without my knowledge. We would stop to see his "family" during these trips, but only for a few hours then get back on the road. His daughter lived in New Castle, PA. So, we stopped there a few times.

Ginger: WHOA!

Glynn: Are you sure? What evidence do you have to support that feeling?

Phoenix: Really, Glynn?!? Are you seriously questioning my integrity? This is why most people don't tell anyone what has happened to them. There is always doubt. If your own family and friends don't believe you; who else will. Luckily, I have proof, asshole! According to a report in a Michigan newspaper, Chris and 17 people were under investigation for about a year and a half when the Feds arrested him and one other person in LaSalle County Illinois. They were on their way back from Texas when they were stopped with $20,000.00 in cash and an undisclosed amount of drugs in their 18-wheeler. This was just three days before we were scheduled to go white water rafting with my mother. Even though I did not want him to go due to us not being

7

together anymore. My mother insisted he was going. Oh well, the Feds took care of that for me. I just texted you the article to read for yourselves:

"Seventeen people in four states have been indicted by a federal grand jury in Pittsburgh on charges of violating federal narcotics, money laundering and postal laws, United States Attorney Scott W. Brady announced today. The three separate, but related, indictments were returned on May 8, 2019, and unsealed this week. "This is one of the largest cocaine distribution rings in western Pennsylvania," said U.S. Attorney Brady. "Together with our state and local law enforcement partners, we conducted an extensive investigation of this multi-state drug distribution network. a third indictment returned on May 8 and containing two counts names. Christopher Weaver, 47, of Pontiac, Michigan, as the sole defendant. Weaver was already in custody. According to the Indictment, from in and around August 2018, and continuing thereafter to in and around September 2018, Weaver conspired with others to distribute and possess with intent to distribute 500 grams or more of cocaine, a Schedule II controlled substance. Additionally, on or about September 17, 2018, Weaver attempted to distribute and possess with intent to distribute 500 grams or more of cocaine, a Schedule II controlled substance. The law provides for a maximum total sentence of not less than five years to a maximum of 40 years in prison, a fine not to exceed $5,000,000 or both."

Phoenix: Wow, you two are so quiet! This is unlike you, Ginger.

DON'T BELIEVE YOUR LYING EYES

Ginger: I'm trying to pick my mouth up off of the floor!

Phoenix: I know right! This shit is better than fiction.

Glynn: So, wait. He was *you* tested, and mother approved?

Phoenix: [Half heartedly laughing] Right! Now do you believe me, Glynn? My mother is a whole neither story. But we did argue about him going or not going. I was like, "we are *not* together." She was like, "So I want him to go." I was like, "Why?" She said, "Because I want him to and I'm paying for the trip, so he is going." Well, that was that. In my head, I was thinking *you bitch!*

Glynn: So, did he coerce her in any way? Or was it his charms she was enamored by?

Phoenix: I have no clue what this man did to my mother. Normally she doesn't like any of my boyfriends. But he was the sun and moon in my mother's eyes. Sometimes I thought she wanted him for herself. I recall a time we were at her house and she told Chris and I that she had cheated on my father during the entire relationship. I meant, what the fuck! You felt a need to say this for the first time in front of *my* boyfriend?

Glynn: Well, that's gross. So, how did she take having her vicarious man-boo getting picked up by the Feds? Did she profess his innocence?

Phoenix: Please, my mother loves that type of stuff. She was mad because she wasted her money paying for his activities. That's what her butt gets for going against her own child.

Glynn: Well, it seems as though there was a delusional idea of who he really was on her end. Still, that doesn't answer the question of if it shattered her perception of him. Was she upset that she had been fooled? Or was it merely frustration at the wasted expense on her dime?

Phoenix: No, her perception was not shattered. They would talk about his past life and how his new life would be different from the fast money lifestyle he was used to. See, my mother dated drug dealers when she was younger. She likes fast money as well. So, Chris was right up her alley.

Glynn: Dag, that's messed up though. So, she didn't even flinch at the charges he was facing?

Phoenix: Nope!

Glynn: Woooooooooow!! Phoenix: Welcome to my life!

Ginger: WOW! I have SO many questions about your mom, but, let's go back a bit. I see drug trafficking and that's a whole story by itself. Other than the Love Bombing, how did he show his narcissism during your relationship? What made him a narc?

Phoenix: It started slowly with little comments about my clothes. He would frown up his face and ask, "Are you wearing that!" or "That don't fit you right." Then once we moved in together; it was small arguments and name-calling. Well, not name-calling but saying things like "you're stupid," "did you really do that," or "I thought you were smarter than that."

Glynn: I have heard versions of that before. Something along the lines of, "Who does that?" or "Oh my god, that's common sense," "You don't know [insert example here]? Everyone knows that," and the like. It is a verbal tactic used to support their behavior and/or diminish your intelligence and decision-making ability. This is done so that you doubt yourself, and have to defer to them.

Ginger: I've experienced those same types of "jabs". He once told me I "need to put my degree on the shelf," implying that I was stupid and undeserving of a college degree.

Phoenix: So, you both know what I mean. Chris even had the nerve to tell me I wasn't smarter than him. Hearing these things from him and my dissertation chair slamming me every chance she got really played on my self-esteem. I was smoking cigarettes and weed like crazy. I was losing weight. I think my hair was even shedding.

Ginger: They're so subtle but deadly! I call it "death by a thousand cuts!" They cause so much strife! It's exhausting.

Glynn: It is imperative that he had you isolated. The more stress in your life, the more likely he could insert himself unnoticed. In this case, it appears as though he was using the stress of your dissertation as a means to cause and "fix" more stress. As if he is the catalyst and solution to all your problems.

Ginger: You nailed it, Glynn. I'm sure there was more, Phoenix.

Phoenix: Isolation! This muthafucka moved me into his family's house next to an abandoned house and two more houses across the street that were destroyed by fire. My friends and family were afraid to come to the house at night because the block looked so spooky. He did not want me to have company when he was not home. He tried to lock me in the house by taking the key to the

11

security door. I told him he was out of his mind if he thought I was going to be locked in the house for hours.

Glynn: Yeah, that is definitely isolated.

Phoenix: Then I noticed small items were missing from the house. Like forks, dishes; then my shoes, hats, and purses. Come to find out, one of his sisters had a key to the house and was stealing my shit every time we left the house.

Ginger: OMGGGGGG! What did you do?

Phoenix: I told him if my shit was not back in this house within 24 hours, I was going to bomb his mother's house, cut his balls off and feed them to him.

Ginger: Hmmm, that sounds reasonable!

Phoenix: I had my shit back six hours later. We changed the locks as well. He acted like he had no clue she was doing these things. He even said he had stuff missing too. But he couldn't say what was missing.

Ginger: He didn't know? So, was Chris on your side about this or did he make excuses?

Phoenix: He was on my side. But he was also involved. He called his step-mother; his step-sister's mother, every time we left the house. I never questioned why he called her, but I know now.

Glynn: And therein lies the manipulation. You came to him with a problem in which he was connected in some way. You let him know that there would be consequences if he did not correct it. And his response? Handle the matter for you, therefore letting you believe that your *insistence* played a role in resolving the issue. When in fact, it may have just been he was waiting on you to notice the items were missing, so that he could swoop in and save the day.

Phoenix: Right! That hero crap!

Ginger: Sonofabitch!! Glynn, you just described the "Good Samaritan" narcissist.

Glynn: Honestly, it comes off as overly elaborate. But I have similar experiences. So, yeah it seems about right.

Phoenix: Good Samaritan my ass! How about one day he hid my cell phone and said I must have misplaced it. So, I'm looking for my phone and find it in his jeans pocket. So, I took the phone and told him I still could not find it. He looked for the phone for hours as I sat at the dining room table unbothered. You see, it was not where he put it. I laughed silently as I watched him. He was so frantic. After this, I knew what and who I was dealing with. I began to make my plan to exit the relationship.

Ginger: The Art of GASLIGHTING! You gave him his own taste. [hitting my knee and laughing]

Glynn: The amount of psychological gymnastics involved is exhausting. It should be an Olympic event. And medals should be given out in the form of professional delousing for those who need to escape these parasites.

Ginger: Psychological gymnastics? That's deep because it's so true! Wow! These parasites, as you appropriately call them, are diabolical in nature! So, Phoenix, what about other things like

13

cheating or triangulation? Did you ever experience that with Chris?

Phoenix: Cheating! He maintained his dating page and would talk to women all the time. He never put his phone down or let me see it. I would see him chatting with other women but he said they were his cousins. Like I'm stupid. You're chatting with your cousin at 2 o'clock in the morning? So, I started cheating. And his entire family was part of the triangulation. His father was the only person who told me, "If I were you I would leave him." He always asked me why I was with Chris. His father and I would have stimulating conversations about life. But he has two wives himself.

Glynn: I was going to say that cheating becomes morally ambiguous in situations such as these. It is a matter of pathos vs ethos. You know it to be wrong, but what you're feeling validates your want to escape; you breakaway by breaking the rules established in the relationship. Thing is, this can be used against you if *you* are caught. Because it no longer focuses on the infidelity that leads you to commit such an act of your own. Rather, it is now just about the act you committed. And this can go the same way if you catch them cheating without having done so yourself.

Ginger: Absolutely! After a while, you pick up their traits or you decide to "get even" and reverse roles. But then you run the risk of retaliation and, face it, you will lose because you don't have the same amount of narcissistic expertise as they do!

Glynn: Or the energy.

Ginger: They are master manipulators. They will always win the manipulation battle. But, going back a bit to what you were saying about family, Phoenix. You know they have their "flying monkeys" to help do their dirty work. It's usually their family or close friends.

Glynn: Or in some cases, YOUR friends or family. Albeit unwittingly, but not always.

Phoenix: Yes, his nephew was his greatest flying monkey. He co-signed every word. One day his nephew came over unannounced to the new house (we moved from his family's home to my family home) to pick up the dog. Oh, yeah, his step-brother asked us to keep his dog for a while. I told his nephew to get the fuck off my porch before I call the police and stop banging on my door. He told me, "My uncle told me you were crazy." I said, "But you are the one on my porch uninvited and banging on my door, and I'm the crazy one?" I closed my blinds and went to watch tv as he sat in my driveway for over 30-minutes. You see, Chris had already moved out and asked me to keep the dog. I called Chris and told him I was going to call the police on his nephew. His nephew left within 5-minutes of us hanging up the phone. Chris apologized for his nephew's behavior and said he did not have him come to the house. He acted shocked and angry. I told him to come get this dog; as he was using him as a way to stay connected to me.

Ginger: They do that often! Mine tried to use my home for storage so he could come back any time he pleased! It was quite obvious. He'd leave anything of value. I finally caught on.

15

Glynn: Speaking on that, so he used his stuff to create Triangulation? I thought that only worked with them using other people, or whatever. Can you elaborate a bit?

Ginger: No, triangulation involves other people; not objects. He kept pieces of himself at my home so he could return. They never want it to end! They keep "portals" open and accessible; little demons.

Glynn: I see. So does it work in the inverse? Do they withhold things of yours, or claim that you have property there that requires your retrieval?

Phoenix: I think there needs to be new studies on triangulation. These mofos are inventing new tactics every day.

Ginger: They'll use any trick that they can!

Phoenix: Right! Like keeping their clothes at your house until they find a place to stay. Thinking they can come over when they need a new outfit.

Glynn: That adds up. I have been contacted regarding things as trivial as socks and chapstick. All in an attempt to lure me back over there, and then pull me into an argument. An argument that wasn't started by me, but was apparently my fault. And if I didn't take the bait, then I would receive notice of an unwanted visit with my items to be dropped off.

Phoenix: It's all about control!

Ginger: Yes! They want to continue the abuse. Getting "supply" from you is their entire mission.

Phoenix: [with tears welling] It took me six months to end this relationship with careful planning and the help of my friends supporting me. I had lost weight from a size 14 to a size 5 in three months. My skin looked horrible and my confidence was low. I did not believe the things that were right in front of my eyes. I was hoping Chris would change and we could be happy together. I realized this was all part of his game. And he played it well.

Glynn: That is the issue that I find fascinating; wanting to change them for the better. I have often been of the mindset that if I could just put more effort into the situation, or just adapt to what is asked of me, then we would work with no problem. The problem is, there was never any consistency for which to correlate. I can do no right. And any wrong I am accused of, I am also chastised for it.

Ginger: Change? They don't need to change. They are perfect beings. In their mind.

Phoenix: True that! They can change; *if* they want to. They have to want to change. But most narcissists do not see themselves as having the problem. It is always someone else's fault for *they* are never wrong.

Ginger: Absolutely! So it's a waste of time to try to convince them that there's a problem unless the problem is YOU!

Phoenix: [laughing] Absolutely!

Glynn: And see you make another good point. When YOU think YOU'RE the problem. Then you become obsessed with improving yourself based on what they tell you is wrong with you. It's as if your capacity to empathize is turned in on itself. Your emotions are used as weapons against you. When really, it's just verbal put-downs. I ended up believing that I was a piece of shit. Honestly, I still kind of do. And in spite of this, there is an annoying part of me that won't stop loving her.

Ginger: So, Glynn, it appears that you are a victim of what I touched on earlier...Gaslighting! It's a form of manipulation where the narcissist tries to alter your reality. Up is down, in is out, black is white. You start to question your own sanity and self-worth. They try to make you believe that you're nuts. It's subtle as well. Once, the batteries from my thermostat were missing. I asked repeatedly about where the batteries were. No one else could have taken them. DeWayne denied it. I finally figured out that he knew I was tired and ready to be done with the relationship. He took the batteries and my heat went out. Then, being a great home improvement guy and the "Good Samaritan," he "fixed" my furnace. He made comments about how warm the house felt, finally! I couldn't believe it. He would do all sorts of things to cause me to question my sanity and to lower my self-esteem. At one point, I actually said out loud, "I feel like I'm in the Twilight Zone"; to which he responded, "So do I!"

Phoenix: That is part of the psychological ambushing and manipulative behavior. They will try to destroy your self-esteem with their abusive words and actions. You begin to think you are the problem and feel like if you change then they will change and the love will flow. But, that is a lie! That will only empower the narc. They will view this as a sign of weakness on the other person's part.

Glynn: Well, damn. . . You're right. And with that in mind, how can I ever be good enough?

Phoenix: Wow, Glynn! She has really done a number on you. Your confidence is way down. You are good enough. No one is good enough in the eyes of a narc.

Glynn: That is who I was referring to; her perception of me. It just sucks, because in my case, we have a kid together. So now my child's perception of me is liable to reflect hers [sighs].

Ginger: You are clearly a victim of narcissistic abuse. The signs that you exhibit are classic. Just to see how much you value her perception of you shows the type of control she has over you. THIS IS NOT YOUR FAULT! No one can be prepared for this type of psychological trauma. In essence, you have a form of PTSD. But make no mistake about it! YOU ARE GOOD ENOUGH!

Phoenix: I understand how you feel, Glynn. I can recall one day, sitting at my computer working on my dissertation and feeling very low about myself. I wondered if I was good enough. I felt trapped in my own body. I remember getting up from my chair, walking to the window, and saying, "I need to get out of here!" But I was looking down at myself; like an out-of-body experience. I did not feel like myself. It felt like someone else had invaded my soul and was controlling my body, thoughts, and actions. I just fell to the floor in tears. I could not believe that this was my life. I knew I had to do something. But what?

FLAME THROWER

Ginger: JESUS CHRIST! Not again, muthaphukka!!!

Phoenix: Oh lawd, now what?

Ginger: He's back! With the Love Bomb from heaven!

Phoenix: Girl, he never left! What are you talking about?

Ginger: I was FREE! Done! FINISHED! WTF is this?

Phoenix: You should see my face.

Ginger: He sounds so sincere, I think he might mean it this time.

Phoenix: Yeah right! Don't fall for the bull! Glynn: So he hit you with a Love Bomb? How so?

Ginger: He said he had an epiphany… a revelation. He now knows where he went wrong. He can't live without me.

Phoenix: Wait, wait, wait…he said he went wrong?

Ginger: Yes!

Phoenix: He knew he fucked up and would say anything! That funky BASTARD.

Glynn: I am sorry. I am still trying to understand this… He actually admitted fault? Was he possessed momentarily by the ghost of a sane person?

Phoenix: [laughing and holding my stomach] I can't!

Ginger: Pssh! This fake epiphany and "moment of clarity" are brought to you by bullshit!!

Glynn: [laughs] BULLSHIT!! Serving you the same stank, since day one.

Ginger: Oh PUH-LEEZ! Ohhh, the almighty LOVE BOMB! PHASE ONE!

Phoenix: Ahh, yes, love bombing. The most important secret weapon of a narc. An attempt to influence you by giving extra attention and affection to gain your love and trust. It could be compliments, promises of the future, or flattery. Even awesome mind-blowing sex!

Ginger: Yes! They tell you everything you want to hear. All of those things that you complained that they weren't doing. They're doing them now! Flowers? You want flowers? Here's 6 dozen roses...every day for a week! Foot massages, date nights, glorious sex, poetry; all of your heart's desires... RIGHT HERE! Right now!

Glynn: What you guys are describing is a little different for me. She would use alluring seduction, family participation, surprise parties; all things that kind of put me in the position to view her as "the one". Inclusion with the intent to isolate. It left me feeling like I owed her my love, my attention, my affection, and my time. And with every minor or major gesture, I was becoming more indebted to her "love".

Phoenix: What type of things would Simone do?

Glynn: There were two separate occasions where she threw me a surprise party. She planned, financed, and even got all my friends to keep it a secret from me. What was messed up about it was that my friends had never done anything like that before. So when I arrived and everyone there yelled, "Surprise!" I thought it was them throwing it for me. Simone wasn't there at the moment, arriving fashionably late, so I had no reason to believe it was her doing. But everyone there made sure to give her the credit.

Ginger: Oh, she was getting the credit! [laughs]

Glynn: EXACTLY!! Not ONE of my friends took credit. And so my event became partially about her. To the extent that now all of my friends in attendance believed that she was "owed my love," too.

Ginger: Partially? [laughs] The ENTIRE EVENT was about her!

Glynn: Pretty much. Featuring me.

Phoenix: That's that attention-seeking b.s. I'm talkin 'bout!

Glynn: It was like everyone there was just promoting how great she was. And I was the only one dating her. No one knew her well enough to draw that conclusion. Yet, here they were. Turning a party for my birthday into like a "pre-engagement party". But it didn't feel... right. I wasn't sure if I should be with her, but here are all my friends advocating for her. And we had been dating for a year at this time, so it seemed like that was the appropriate thing to do. It felt like I was being led this way against my will. Manipulated by those closest to me. My mother and step-father were there, friends I grew up with, people who didn't show were calling. The odd thing was, none of my female friends were there. I am sure it was by design. On the one hand, she wasn't acquainted with them. On the other hand, I am sure she would not want them there even if she was.

Phoenix: So, exactly what happened at the party? And was your boy there? You know! The one she slept with? I don't know how you stayed with that trick after that crap?

Ginger: Phoenix, I don't know either! But those master manipulators have an "APP" for everything. So what happened?

Glynn: Interesting you would bring that up. Yes, actually. Tre was there. At the time of this party, I was only privy to the knowledge that they had a one-night stand before we began dating. Something that ate away at me due to something you guys had mentioned previously; Triangulation? Tre and I had been childhood friends, so we hung out a lot. That said, him being there felt odd to me. Seemed like a non-issue at the moment. He was there with two different women; one at the beginning of the night, and one toward the middle. By the end of the night, he had none. The biggest surprise came later that evening, when the future wife of Tre, Camille, caught him making a pass on the hostess of the party, my Simone.

Ginger: Glynn, hold on. I have a couple of questions. You dated her after Tre? How did that happen?

Glynn: No, they hadn't dated at that time. They were only friends that had slept together once.

Phoenix: Wait! What happened? He was hitting on Simone after bringing two other females to YOUR party? Then having his main girl come later? Am I understanding this correctly?

Glynn: YES!! Not gonna lie, part of me used to respect when he did that kind of pimp move back when we were younger. I've since outgrown that way of thinking. Camille left the party in a huff and didn't reveal anything to anyone. [sighs] And the rest of the night went on without incident. You would think that at some point Simone would tell me what happened. Pull me aside maybe, or even wait until the party had ended. I didn't find out any of this until three years later. Knowing that now, and everything that followed, it taints every gesture of love that she shared with me.

Phoenix: So, after finding out all that; you still decided to stay with her. What was on your mind my friend? Was the box that good? [laughing uncontrollably with tears in her eyes]

Glynn: Ha!! Funny. It wasn't that. It was a matter of conflicting views interfering in my decision making.

Ginger: What do you mean by conflicting views? I don't understand.

Glynn: Umm...my long time friends would say that I was being a bit paranoid. Like, I was tripping to have any concerns. Their "advice" was to stay or go. Which seemed solid at the time. Though this wasn't the case. First, Tre was one of my "friends" giving this advice. And second, she had been talking to my friends behind my back. They had been leaking information about the conversations that we had regarding my frustrations.

Phoenix: So, Simone formed an alliance with your friends?

Glynn: More like a coalition. It got to the point where if you had a dick, I didn't trust what you had to say. You might be compromised. Which was the opposite for her, because she didn't want any vaginas in my ear giving me a counter perspective. As long as I was being spoon-fed what she wanted me to know, then I can remain ignorant and malleable.

Phoenix: This is the same chick you were dating when we worked at American Mental Health Services. Dude, you were having problems then! What the fuck!

Glynn: Yes, I was unaccustomed to working with an office full of women. And I was afraid to discuss it with you and the other ladies at work. I felt like I was betraying her by sharing personal information about our relationship. Even though there was no ulterior motive, just genuine concern, you all were a threat to us.

Phoenix: I can see how she may have felt that way. But I think her emotions or way of thinking was more about controlling you. Telling you who you could or could not be friends with. I remember us walking to Bellacino's one day and you telling me about her controlling behavior. I think I told you then that she was going to be a problem and to GET OUT of the relationship. Shout out to Jordan Peele! [laughing out loud]

Glynn: [chuckles] This is true, but also the kind of talk that lends itself to her line of thinking. Thing is, her logic was that everyone in the office wanted the "D." Probably to play into my ego a bit. That wasn't how I saw any of you though, so that didn't work too well. But with so many women advising me to leave her alone, it did lend some legitimacy to her theory about sabotaging our relationship.

Ginger: That's how they use your words against you.

Phoenix: Umm-hmm. I remember you saying she would question your intelligence and your use of "big" words. Didn't she say you thought you were better than other people?

Glynn: [scoffs] Question it? She would downright hold an inquisition to prove that my vocabulary and way of speaking was just a means to be condescending. As if my intellect was entirely predicated on the notion that I had some absurd obsession with proving I was somehow superior to others. Funny thing is, it was basically a projection on her end.

Phoenix: Ooooooo, projection! I like that! So, are you saying that she may have felt inferior to you or your extensive vocabulary or that you made her feel stupid?

Glynn: Yeah, but it is more than that. Let's say we were having an argument. As a means of clotting my thoughts, she would berate me into saying things I hadn't thought through thoroughly. Or if I took the time to *properly* express a thought, then I was taking too long. It was frustrating and exhausting. I couldn't construct a proper sentence without it being scrutinized by false logic and duplicitous rationale.

Phoenix: It sounds like she was trying to keep you off balance by not allowing you to think but only react to situations she created.

Ginger: Yes, it's another tactic they use to cause you to question your sanity and intelligence. Mine always took everything I said and picked it apart; word for word. Any error or loophole, he pounced. I finally learned to give him NOTHING! I even stopped admitting fault. I didn't care what it was...I gave him NOTHING!

Glynn: It's like verbal Judo. The only way to engage or to win is to use verbal Jiu-Jitsu, and go to the ground with her and wrestle it out. But it doesn't matter the outcome, she will still determine herself the victor.

Ginger: I don't understand how she figured she was the victor, other than trying to find a way to boost her incredibly low self-esteem, which is ultimately their biggest issue.

Glynn: Neither do I, but I can give you an example. After I found evidence by going through her phone-- [sighs] Something I am not very proud of, mind you. I discovered text with pictures of Tre's dick, amongst some other questionable messages, and I confronted her about it. She made the argument about me knowing her passcode and going through her phone.

Ginger: HA! Classic deflection! "Hey, I just found out that you sucked Tre's cock." "WHAT??? How DARE you look at the video on my phone showing me sucking Tre's cock. You've violated my privacy!" Nahhhh, bitch! HE violated your privacy when he put his cock in your mouth!

Glynn: [laughs] Pretty much. For the sake of context though I feel I should add that I only went through her phone because she went through mine on a couple of separate occasions. But that moment revealed so much. We argued all night. And I didn't receive an apology for her transgressions.

Ginger: What transgressions? They're never wrong!

Phoenix: You actually expected an apology?

Glynn: It ain't even about the right or wrong of it. It was about the hurt.

Phoenix: Your hurt IS their supply! I honestly think they get a kick from your pain.

Ginger: Exactly! That's why I would desperately try to give him NOTHING! I could be half-dead and would spruce up when he came around. He would NEVER see me sweat...until... He pushed EVERY BUTTON on my mental elevator!

Phoenix: And it is rare that these assholes will apologize since nothing is their fault.

Glynn: Well, I got a shallow one... eventually. And even that one got rescinded over the years. At this point, not only is she not sorry but she told me she didn't even owe me honesty about sleeping around. I, to this day, can't make sense of it. All that time spent was just transactional I guess. Ugh!! I was asked repeatedly, why didn't I leave sooner? Why did I stay and have a kid with her? But I had already invested so much of myself into her and her family; she has three kids I bonded with over the years. What do you do when you have been conditioned to serve as a surrogate father, in a family where the matriarch sees you as disposable?

Phoenix: It sounds like you had more of an attachment to her children. Where are her other babies' dads? I wonder if they experienced what you did and got the fuck out of dodge? Chris tried to use his mother and my mother to continue our relationship. I was not having that shit!

Glynn: Her other children's fathers were around until they weren't. So it is definitely a good chance that they became less active when I came around. But honestly, I only ever met them like a couple of times or so. That in of itself is some Grade A, BS. She would bad mouth them, and praise how I am with her kids. That all stopped once we had a child. Now I am apparently the worst father ever. And any credibility I built over the years by being there and doing dad shit is reduced to zero. Meanwhile, her other baby daddies are now leagues above me. Even though they are more mythological than actual at this point. I mean I hear about them, but I have yet to see them do anything fatherly myself. One of them gave me money to give to his boys as a gift because he *knew* she would not let them accept it if he gave it to them himself. And he was right. She found the money in the boy's room one day (I guess one of them had let it slip they had it), and she called me to yell at me for giving it to them. She said I was out of line. She also said I should have told her and gave her the money. I asked what she would have done with it if I did give it to her. She responded with, "I would have given it right back to his punk ass!" Thing is, that was the one time I actually felt bad for one of her other kid's fathers. I saw how the whole thing played out that day. He came to town for a visit. The whole time she was giving him hell over the phone for a bunch of stuff that I was not entirely clear about. When he showed up, she was dead silent for the duration of his visit. It made things pretty awkward. That's why he asked me to give them the cash gift. It seemed like a bum move, but I could tell he was just kind of over it. And what's worse, I know how he felt. Simone has this whole "Get Over It" attitude. So she will berate you, in front of other people-- embarrassing you—and expect you to carry on like nothing happened. And you BETTER not call her out on that shit, or you'll come looking like the crazy person. She uses her femininity and motherhood status to villainize you when you don't cooperate. Of course, this is only applicable to the men in her life. For women, she uses another kind of intimidation tactic.

Ginger: Sometimes, when I listen to these stories of what has happened to many people who are victimized by these maggots, I wonder if they've been listening in on conversations that I've had with DeWayne. There's NO WAY that these stories can be so closely aligned...and then I remember! They all operate from the exact same playbook...with little twists here and there, but the gist of their craziness is about the same!

Glynn: Tell me, did DeWayne ever use the reverse victim play? Where he claimed *he* was actually the one who has been victimized? Then he says you always play the victim but in actuality, it's just that he wronged you?

Ginger: Yep! DeWayne would do some really foul shit and when he would see me reaching my breaking point, he would hit me with the love-bombing apology and epiphany. And when I'd take him back, he'd somehow blame me for what happened. Or, he'd discard me first and give me the silent treatment!!! OMG! That dreaded SILENT TREATMENT!

Glynn: The silent treatment!! Classic! Simone pulled that shit constantly. But the difference is, she would call me first to force an argument. Then, she would hang up mid-argument to provoke me into trying to reach out to her. If I didn't, then I was in the wrong for not pestering her and would be punished for it further. So it comes off like a self-imposed silent treatment. That is the mental mind fuckery of it all; the ability to turn everything back on you. Like every terrible act is your fault, and. . . they don't know how to be held accountable for anything! Even if Simone admitted guilt, there was always a caveat. And she was never ashamed. It is self-indulgent juvenile behavior with the intent to break your logic center. And, drive you to accept whatever nonsense they decide to throw at you. It's Gaslighting! But aggressive and offensive. More like Flamethrowing; trying to burn away any common sense with irrational vitriol. Gawd!! Damn it!! It pisses me off just thinking about it.

Phoenix: Speaking of the silent treatment. Yesterday was lil man's birthday. Were you able to help plan or attend his birthday celebration?

Glynn: Yeah, I wasn't invited to that. So let's leave it at that for now.

Ginger: I'm sorry! WHAT?

Phoenix: Wow! That's fucked up. I know you must be feeling some kind of way.

Glynn: Every kind of way. But that is standard. Right now I feel at fault. It's messed up! But I expected it.

Phoenix: Your fault? What do you mean by that?

Glynn: It's like the "Flamethrowing" term I used earlier. All the logical notions were burned away by the anxiety and mental/emotional abuse. So I am left with no defense, engulfed by the ire my Emotional Immune System was keeping at bay. It doesn't make sense in my head but I feel all of this negative energy. Even when she isn't present to inflict it. Like a Phantom of Guilt reinforcing all the errors I have amounted as a father. Most notably my lack of presence. Ugh. . .

Ginger: Lawd! Simone sucks the energy out of me! I can only imagine how you're suffering!

Phoenix: I empathize with your frustration. But it's kind of hard to be a parent when the other party is putting up barriers and sabotaging your relationship with your son. You tried making mutual plans to spend time with him. But Simone changes the time or rejected your visits if you are a minute late. My only suggestion is taking her to court for visitation rights as a father. I'm just glad I can be here for you as a friend. As a male, it can be hard to express your feelings without feeling judged or viewed as weak. But males experience toxic relationships too!

Glynn: THAT!! THAT RIGHT THERE!! The toxicity is such that it is hard to express anything without coming off like I am whining. Even if I have a valid example of abuse, time apparently overrides it. It becomes a claim of victimhood that I apparently didn't earn. Something that was under a statute of limitations, which expires at any indiscriminate moment. I appreciate you as my friend. Everyone else seems to be under her cerebral conditioning, so they don't appear to be helpful. Actually, they seem to be more on her side.

Ginger: Sounds like her "flying monkey" tactic has been activated! ABUSE by PROXY; using your "friends" and some family.

Phoenix: It seems like she is trying to isolate you from your friends and family. I know your mother has been trippin' and playing it neutral until recently. I can't understand why as a mother and woman, she can't see through Simone's manipulation. It's like... she is drinking the Kool-Aid of deception. You know...it's really hard when your family and friends don't support you. I remember one time I called my mother for help. I told her I didn't feel safe and needed her help in getting out of the house and the relationship. She came over and just sat in the kitchen and talked to both of us. Chris was like... "I feel like I've been set up. I think you are going to leave me." Well...that was the plan. But that was not the case that day. I was trying to tell her discreetly I wanted to leave but she just didn't get it. At that point, I knew I couldn't even trust MY OWN MOTHER. But I should have expected as much as my mother has never been much of an emotional support for me. But that is a story for another day. Oy vey!

Glynn: I would say that my son is the only reason the manipulation is possible. Without him, there would be no reason for them to interact with one another. Hell, my mom was the one that was advocating for me to cut ties with her. My response would often be that I felt some kind of obligation to stay due to the bond I built over the years with Simone's other children. I had been there for years and assisted in raising those kids. Though if you ask Simone, I ain't do shit. I showed them how to ride bikes, taught them about nature, and explained to them how to cook certain dishes. I was co-parenting before I even became a father. Which, at the time, it was my mother who made me aware that she might be using the kids to manipulate me; another example of triangulation. I didn't believe her at the time, because I thought Simone was better than that. Low and behold my mother was right! I figured out what was going on too late. Problem is, now the manipulation is on the other foot. Now that we have a child together, she doesn't need to use her other children. She has even gone as far as to try to cover my communication with my son's siblings. Instead, she uses our son to manipulate and triangulate my mother. And my mom can't even see it. It's at the point where even when I break it down and explain to my mother how Simone is doing it; my mother refuses to believe that she is being manipulated. She stands firm in the belief that she is making all her own decisions, uninfluenced. But if ever my mom does side with me, Simone tries to use *me* to punish my own mother. SHIT IS CRAZY!!

Ginger: Fortunately for me, DeWayne lives very close to my sister and my family could see who he was; probably before I did. We all kind of figured out what I was dealing with. They've been very supportive. But, initially, my mom was excited that I had finally found a "good man" and hoped that I didn't "mess it up"! [laughs] Ma'am, I've NEVER been the toxic one. I'm selected to be the victim from when my empathic ass first opens my mouth. These predators hunt us, study us, know us better than we know ourselves. DeWayne actually told me that he has studied me and knows my next move before I do. It's crazy how they operate and manipulate. But, if you don't know who they actually are, you would think I was lying and you would hang on to their every word. I used to tell DeWayne that he had the "gift to gab" and could talk his way out of a DNA test. During arguments, I would retreat because his points seemed so valid by the time he finished twisting them. I didn't know that he was gaslighting me, but I knew I was being manipulated. I just didn't understand for the life of me WHY I would allow it. I'm super intelligent and highly educated. I even graduated in psychology. How was I allowing this to happen? It was like I was under a spell. I'm still embarrassed by my behavior. So I get it, Glynn. I often blame myself for being a victim of narcissistic abuse. In fact, I'm still being abused by Dewayne. Sometimes I feel trapped, even though I know I am not. I can take a hard NO stance and keep him away from me, but like 'battered wives syndrome', I feel stuck! Right now, I am financially strapped and he helps me with those extra straws that might break my back. Many call it an excuse...Maybe it is, but until you live my life, don't make decisions that you deem are best for me. Right now, I feel that I don't really have much of a choice. Being a slave to finances is why I'm in this shit now. I really need to do better. Anyway, about to hit the casino. [laughing out loud]

Phoenix: First off, I'm in tears with laughter about DeWayne "could talk his way out of a DNA test!" But that's a part of the appeal of their charm. And for some, it's their striking good looks. They will prey on your empathy and sympathy to woo you over. Then once you are in their clutches, they will exploit your vulnerabilities, rake you over the coals with your family and friends, then leave you rode hard and put up wet in a state of mental confusion. I don't know if the shame and guilt of allowing yourself to be so submissive are worse for a male or a female, but it seems like the end result is the same. You feel broken, weak, and exhausted. Like no one understands what you are going through because this type of individual will have the WORLD thinking you are to blame and they are the victim. But once in this toxic relationship you are either a conscious player or blind-sided into it by their cliff-hanging or stonewalling tactics. For the victim, it could take months, even years to realize what is going on. Exiting the relationship takes careful planning and a strong will to want to be freed from this type of uncanny abuse. I am pooped by just talking about it. I think I'm getting a headache. But it's amazing how a TRUE narcissist will play on your compassion as a human being, distort the truth, leave out their role in the situation, and orchestrate the narrative in their favor. I mean, you can't make this shit up. When they say the truth is stranger than fiction, they didn't lie! Oh, shoot! I'm getting another call. Hold on y'all.

Phoenix clicks to the other line. Phoenix: Hello!

FLIP..THAT...NARC

As Phoenix has Glynn and Ginger on hold:

Ginger: I think I met my soulmate, y'all. He's charming, loving, caring, considerate, has his own company, delightful, and cute. Wow! He's all that I'm looking for. Dewayne Coleman...Such a delightful man. Yeah, I'm marrying this dude. Did anyone of y'all feel like that? DeWayne swept me off my feet. He knew what I was thinking; would finish my sentences; would leave beautiful messages...and I ATE IT UP. I was in the process of moving to Atlanta where my brother and sister had moved to. During a visit, I met DeWayne, who lives close to my sister - on the same block. He had a handsome young son who played with my nieces every day. DeWayne was outside one day and started speaking to my sister, who introduced us. She asked if he wanted to come over to play cards that evening. He accepted. We had a great time. Then my sister and husband retired to their bedroom. DeWayne and I continued playing cards and flirting. I was smitten and he seemed to be, too. I flew back home the next day and we kept in touch. Over the next few months, we grew extremely close and I thought I was in love. DeWayne even helped me finish my Master's paper. I had procrastinated so long on it and he helped me focus. He wouldn't talk to me until I wrote 5 pages a day. Being infatuated, I did just that. By day 6, I was done. I didn't realize that he would eventually take all the credit for me obtaining my Master's Degree. [laughs] But I digress. I finally got the nerve to pack up and go. My daughter in tow, I moved to the ATL!

Phoenix: OMG! I know exactly how you felt. I thought Chris and I were "soulmates". Mind you we met on an online site. So, when I first saw his profile picture I said in my head, "Where have you been all my life." I was literally drawn to this man's picture.

Ginger: And I repeat! You DO KNOW that online dating sites are the narcissists' hunting grounds, right? Those are one of their favorite places to roam. So many victims to choose from. [Shaking my head!]

Phoenix: SHUT UP GINGER.

Glynn: She isn't wrong, though.

Ginger: NO LIE!

Glynn: So we talking soulmates now? Idunno 'bout all that, though.

Phoenix: [laughs] Glynn, do men even think that soulmates exist?

Glynn: Sometimes I think they do, but it is a sparse amount. And out of those who do, their criteria is pretty stacked. I could be wrong, but I never really encountered many men who would use the term freely. Offhand, I can think of only one-- outside of myself, of course. [laughs] I would like to think I am more cautious with that term. I am not sure I would consider Simone my "soulmate". Though, I undoubtedly feel bound to her. And I want to emphasize that difference; I feel "bound to" not "bonded with".

39

Ginger: I consider "bound to" to mean "soul ties". Soul ties are completely different from soulmates. You're essentially tied to her through your souls (unwillingly, in this case).

Glynn: Yeah, I have heard that term before. It definitely feels that way. It's a combination of emotions that amount to this overwhelming feeling of obligation. As if I have to make her happy in order to be happy. Like I can't live without her. It is easy to conflate it with what people often perceive a soulmate to be. Though it may seem involuntary, it is induced behaviour based on emotional manipulation, mental conditioning (or gaslighting), and physical gratification. She will starve me of affection, positive reinforcement, and sex, in what seems like an attempt to make me feel as though I need her. It is similar to drug addiction more than a relationship. . . Hell, I have even had episodes of withdrawal. [chuckles]

Phoenix: Hmmmm? Ginger, how are you and DeWayne doing now?

Ginger: As terrible as ever. He's happy to have me back in his Twilight Zone as he works on my bathroom, doing "ONE" thing every other day, in order to keep his foot in the door. He delights in my misery, so I pretend to be happy, crying inside...Feeling trapped! But as I said, I give him NOTHING to hold against me.

Glynn: Yo, speaking of which, I asked around about that. I heard it should take about two weeks to complete a bathroom remodel.

Ginger: [laughing out loud] NO SHIT!

Glynn: Well, if he keeps pussyfooting around, "YOUR SHIT" is gonna have to be done in an outhouse.

Phoenix: [rolling on the floor laughing with tears in my eyes] Right!!!!

Ginger: [laughing] I was thinking about calling one of those TV shows like "Flip This House" and share my story, praying they'd have sympathy for me. [laughs] His stalling tactics are so evident! How about we start a show called "Flip...That...Narc!!"

Glynn: Ha!!

Phoenix: [holding my stomach laughing] I just can't with you Ginger!

Ginger: Well, that's kind of what happened when I moved. No kidding! Two months after I moved down there, I realized that DeWayne was NOT the soulmate that I thought he was. We had established soul ties and his son had latched on to me and me to him. I was ready to "FLIP THAT NARC". [laughs] But, I didn't know that he was a narc at that time. I could only identify the characteristics. I knew what he was going to do and why he was doing the things that he was doing. I just didn't have a name for it. During my Psychology studies, there wasn't a strong emphasis on Narcissistic Personality Disorder (NPD). Epic fail, in my opinion. These parasites are ruining lives like drug addicts, but lie right under the radar. They need to be exposed!

Glynn: So, DeWayne has a kid too? How old?

Ginger: Yep. He's 18 now. I came into his life at 9. His mother had abandoned ship and remarried. She was not involved at all until she got divorced. That's a whole other story, though. But I raised him until adulthood and beyond. He considers me his mother. I consider him my son. Unfortunately, he's another portal for DeWayne to enter through. What did you call it, Glynn, Psychological gymnastics??? That's my life!

Glynn: Got damn! That's crazy! You hear about father's abandonment so often. But you don't often consider motherly abandonment.

Ginger: I can only imagine that she was beat down from the narcissistic abuse. But I found out later that she had a history of abandonment. I guess childhood trauma caused her to let go so easily. I don't really understand it, myself.

Phoenix: So wait, let's go back. Which behaviors did DeWayne present? I know when you first met him, you met his representative.

Ginger: Whew!!! There are so many. What I described above was the "love bomb" phase. You fall for them, hook, line, and sinker. Then, he activated the devaluation phase. He would give left-handed compliments. For example, he'd say, "I like those shoes, I mean, they'd look better in blue, but I guess green is ok...if you like them." He would insult my intelligence and state, "I know you're smart because you have a degree, but..." Once, we had an argument and he told me that I needed to "put my degree on the shelf". I mentioned this earlier. I said, "Which one! In fact, BOY GENIUS, let's play 'Little Degree Take Big Degree'! Put your biggest degree out there, dude!" [laughs] He didn't like that. I wasn't trying to brag. I was fighting back! He could never say anything complimentary like he did in the love bomb phase. I felt that he was trying to lower my self-esteem and I called him out on it. He would then project and deflect, making everything my fault. His gaslighting or "flame-throwing" as Glynn calls it, was and is overbearing. DeWayne was never happy with my accomplishments, but he'd fake empathy and excitement. When I'd bring good news, he'd kill my excitement by saying, "Not to dull your light, but things like this don't happen for me. God obviously has his favorites."

Glynn: What the-- Really? Yeah, I don't like that.

Phoenix: Most people would ask why stay in such an abusive relationship? But they may have never been with someone who can make you feel like you are the only person in the world and that they will do any and everything to please. At least at the start of the relationship. Their representative is THE SHIT. [half laughing but feeling empty inside] You just learn to roll with the punches as we all did or still do. We begin to play their game. Trying to one-up them with verbal debates.

Ginger: People like me… like us… are empaths. We want to see the best in others. We want to believe in the good of the world. We're optimistic, loving, caring, and considerate. We think that the person who love-bombed us (unsuspectingly) is the real person when it is, in fact, their representative. The real person presents themselves within a few months. Their mask slips and they are revealed. We still pray to see that great person they exhibited in the beginning. HE DOESN'T EXIST!

Phoenix: I think that is part of the draw. We provide so much empathy, encouragement, and support that feeds their narcissistic supply. At times, we will even sacrifice our own happiness and sanity to keep them.

Ginger: Exactly! You hit the nail on the head! NARCISSISTIC SUPPLY! They do all of this to get their supply. It's like oxygen to them. They desperately need it. The more the merrier! The more negative, the better the supply.

Phoenix: Damn, Glynn! You have been soooo quiet. Are you taking notes or something? Or are you identifying with DeWayne? [laughs]

Glynn: I am. . . And I am still sitting here thinking about that 18 years old part. I am trying to figure out how one would separate from someone after being in his life for so long. There are personal reasons for me wanting to know.

Ginger: She left when he was about 6. She returned when he was 14 or so. He, William, has yet to forgive her, but he is dealing with her because she is his biological mother. He lives with me, his momma!

Glynn: Where were you when she returned?

Ginger: We were living together. She came back after her divorce.

Glynn: So, all of you were in the same house; father and son?

Phoenix: How did you get that from the conversation, Glynn? What I heard was Ginger and DeWayne were living together when his ex-wife came back into the picture.

Glynn: I was trying to clarify if William was living with her too. I wasn't sure.

Ginger: And my daughter. She came back to get her man back, I guess. Long story short, I gave him right back to her. [laughs] I just wanted to keep William. It was a brief tug-of-war, but biologically, I knew he wasn't mine and I had no legal rights, so I had to let go. I would call and check on him every Sunday to make sure he was okay. That was the worst part of the breakup. Eventually, they broke it off, which I knew would happen because he was the same person that she divorced. Narcs never change. She was also the same person who abandoned her children. You can't just develop that mother instinct (in my opinion). So, she fell off, too...just not all the way off this time. William said to me, "I'm just waiting on her to leave again." It was sad to hear that. Anyway, after their breakup, William tried so hard to come back to my home.

DeWayne made him (William) leave when I put him out for running around with Amber, his ex-wife. When William tried to come back, DeWayne refused. I think it was because of the no-contact order that I initiated. Anyway, an argument ensued between us and DeWayne told me, in front of William, that I would never see him again. William reacted angrily and they had a physical altercation. I knew DeWayne messed up because William loves me as his mom. After that, the narcissistic silent treatment towards William was activated. He completely stopped parenting. Didn't even provide food. I remember going to the local bulk grocery store and loading up on food for William to have stashed away. One day, William asked to come over. Of course, I let him come for the night. Two years later, he's still here...about to graduate high school and going off to college. I'm so proud of him. But honestly, I think he might have a few "traits" himself. I don't know, but I'm watching. But, I do know that he does not like his father and he doesn't want him anywhere around me!

Phoenix: This is like a soap opera!

Ginger: As the Gaslighting Burns starring DeWayne Coleman and Ginger Harmon.

Glynn: Narcs of Our Lives. . . will return after a brief word from our sponsor. . . Next time on, "Flip That Narc!"

Phoenix: Young and the Narcissist...As the Narcissist Turns.

Ginger: [laughing] EXACTLY! Sometimes I even wonder how the next episode will play out. These nuts are intriguing if nothing else. But that's just some of my experiences with DeWayne. After about a year, he started hoovering me. In fact, the hoover started before a year but intensified over the summer.

Glynn: Is the Hoovering similar to the Love Bombing?

Ginger: No, not really, but it's the prerequisite to the love bomb. The hoover comes from the hoover vacuum cleaner. Hoovering is an attempt to suck you back in. The narcissist might send you a birthday card or text. They might call to check on you or to request an item they left on purpose, just to see how you respond. They feel you out, in a sense, to see if you're receptive to any type of dealings with them. Once you respond, they KNOW that you're still in it. They bide their time and pounce.

Glynn: Does DeWayne ever Hoover or Love Bomb William or your daughter, as a means of getting or luring you back?

Ginger: [laughing] Does he EVER!!! Everyone and everything is used at his disposal. He even uses my cat to get to me! "I brought Grayson some treats. Can I bring them by?" BULLSHIT! YOU NOT! He conditioned my cat to come to him as soon as he comes in the house. Grayson, my little human cat, sees him and runs up to him immediately, knowing that a snack is coming. He'd say to him, "I guess I'm the only one who pays you any attention". But I'll NEVER forget how animals are truly able to feel people. Grayson peed in DeWayne's house-shoe one day. [laughs] I immediately thought to myself, "He knows you're full of shit, too!" Anyway, these tactics are why it's so hard to fight back and going completely NO-CONTACT is imperative. Once you give them a semblance of weakness or acceptance, they squeeze right back in and you're back in the FUNHOUSE where they're the only ones having fun!

Glynn: I don't know how to feel about staying away. In my situation, it doesn't benefit my son for me to stay away. He is showing signs of being the child of a Narcissist by way of his "all about me" temperament. Some people think he is spoiled, and I want to break that behavior.

Ginger: In your situation, you have to use the "Gray Rock" tactic which is similar to No Contact. If it doesn't pertain to your son, there's no conversation to be had.

Phoenix: Wait, let's get back to this hoovering shit. Tell us what happened on your birthday?

Ginger: [rolls eyes] We weren't talking. In fact, it was almost a year of no contact and he was blocked. My mother, acting as an unsuspecting flying monkey, relayed a message to me that DeWayne wished me a happy birthday. We laughed, but I knew that it was a hoover attempt (I had been studying up on narcissism at this point). I knew that he was going to initiate contact soon. I didn't know when. The next month, I was sitting in my car at my sister's house and DeWayne was outside. Something inside said that he was going to say something to me because I saw him looking over my way. I was strong, cocky, ready to slay his narcissistic ass. As soon as I walked up to my sister's house, he intentionally turned to me and spoke. I spoke quickly and reached for the door. Actually, I OPENED a door of unsolicited communication. He jumped at the opportunity. I was ready! He said, "Oh, you're not mad at me anymore? I said, "Nope...never was." He said, "Huh? What did you say? Hold on, I can't hear you. Can I come over to talk to you for a second?" I accepted. I accepted because I had read up on the hoover and I knew how to control and handle this narc. I wasn't worried at all! He rushed over and started talking to me, apologizing for the infidelity, and thanking me for continuing to look out for William. I took it all in, but remained defiant. I had been here before with him. But this time was different. His gift of gab wouldn't work. Say your peace and leave me alone. I'm staying no-contact. He talked and talked. My mind was made up. No amount of apologies, epiphanies, or revelations would change my position on him. He was done! I wanted nothing to do with him and he knew it. After a while, I tried to end the conversation. My tough exterior would not be penetrated. ALAS! Conversation

OVER! DeWayne was now eating my pussy!! WHAT THE FUCK???

Phoenix: Gurrrl, how did you allow that to happen? You know how they will trick you and use manipulation. Well, did he change?

Ginger: YES! In that moment...During the love bomb phase, they are back to their initial representative. He was so loving and showed a different side that I had never seen before. He did a lot of the things that I requested before, showing me that he heard my cries.

Phoenix: Like what? What did he do?

Ginger: He became a hopeless romantic! He was a complete gentleman. He would pay for a lot of things, pretend he was working multiple home improvement jobs, talk about buying a house (again) and a car. You know, "future faking". All he wanted was a "best friend" and he had chosen little old me to fill the position. He wanted to help me fix up my house; remodel the bathroom and kitchen. Any and everything I wanted, he wanted to give me. Essentially and in retrospect, blowing new smoke up my ass. I had heard it before, but I thought the "epiphany" wasn't that. I thought that the literature I read up on was true in many cases, but it was different in DeWayne's case. He has truly seen the err of his ways and his narcissism was kind of "cured". My guard stayed up and he knew it. He stayed as the new and improved DeWayne for about a month. I was proud! My love had changed the narcissist. I had slain the evil narc and restored DeWayne's mental health. With my chest pumped out, I started dropping my guard. Once it was low enough, BOOM! Amber's back and DeWayne was all for it.

Phoenix: No, you began to question yourself. You thought you were wrong about him. Amber was just another piece to feed the narc. But anyway!

Ginger: "WHY is she around now? What does she want?" DeWayne, wanting to "be honest" and tell his "best friend" everything, proceeded to tell me that she needed her brakes changed…"And that concerns you how? You know what," I exclaimed, "You can change her panties if you want to. WHAT THE FUCK!" Here we go!! Triangulation continues…. Next thing you know, Amber's showing up to family events at his mother's house, which was a tell-tale sign before when she showed up to a niece's birthday party. I wasn't for ANY of it. I said, "So, I can cheat on you and the guy I cheated with can pop up whenever and you'll be good with it!" What was his answer? "Well, if it's Sarah's dad, I wouldn't mind!" You are a damn lie! These occurrences continued and then, Amber's older son, Dewayne's stepson, was killed and the saga continued! Help me JESUS!

Glynn: The fuck? Homie, please! That is not remotely true. The only reason he would even say is if he thought that it would make him look like the bigger person in that situation.

Phoenix: Did I hear you right?!?! Amber was showing up to family events that you were NOT invited to? I'm confused. Were you and DeWayne back together at this point? By the way, if the shoe was on the other foot; and Sarah's father was in the picture, DEWAYNE WOULD OF HAD A CONNIPTION.

Ginger: You heard me! Right before they first started running around, she was showing up to events all of a sudden that I wasn't invited to. Then, she was trying to see William a whole lot more. I figured that she was divorced. Because it's public record, I could check and, sure enough, she was. She was implementing her plan to win "her family" back that she abandoned. DeWayne took the bait. After we reconciled, she was showing up and I was there. In a normal circumstance, I wouldn't care because I'm usually very secure in these situations. But after their little stunt, I wasn't for it. We argued often. Then I realized that she was his primary supply, like I was, and the narcissist wanted all of it. He reveled in my agony about Amber's presence. We went back and forth. He made so many excuses and reasons why she was around and why it was necessary. I was baffled. William lived with me. Why did she need to come over to his parents' house (where he currently resides)? At first, I tried to be understanding. They lost a child. But, honestly, I think DeWayne used this as a way to get Amber back. Once again, he was willing to sacrifice it all to have a relationship with Amber. Finally, I decided to get off the triangulation roller coaster. I went off...said FUCK YOU AND FUCK AMBER. Don't say shit else to me. I Rolled out! For good...

Glynn: Wait a minute. You mentioned that they lost a child. But was that before or after their divorce?

Phoenix: I was thinking the same thing! How old is this child and when did they lose him?

Ginger: He was 28. He was killed. It was ruled a suicide, but they don't believe that's what happened. After he died, DeWayne rushed in to save the day.

Phoenix: But that's a hard one to lose a child, Ginger.

Ginger: Oh, I know. It was horrible. After everything that happened, I stood by BOTH of their sides during the entire ordeal. I was actually hurting for them.

Phoenix: You did what?!?!

Ginger: Yes, I was there, supporting DeWayne, Amber, and William. I called Amber almost every day to check on her. Wait, let me give a little background to clear up a few things. After their breakup, Amber reached out to me to apologize for running around with DeWayne and to thank me for looking out for William and DeWayne Jr., their oldest son together. We met at a restaurant and hashed things out. We started co-parenting William because he was still on silent treatment from DeWayne. So, in essence, I was able to forgive and move on. In fact, when their son passed, Amber called me before reaching out to DeWayne. However, after DeWayne and I rekindled and Amber started showing up unannounced to family events, those old feelings rushed back and my guard flew up.

Phoenix: That was very mature of you and Amber. How did DeWayne react to your new-found friendship? Wait, let me get my popcorn. [Phoenix goes to the kitchen to pop some Orville Redenbacher extra butter popcorn and grabs a Pepsi]

Ginger: [laughs] He found out later that William was living with me. He thought William was living with Amber. He confronted Amber (I was still in No-Contact mode). He asked why William was not living with her and why he was at my house. Amber told him "don't worry about it. We got this". This infuriated

DeWayne. He did NOT like us talking and getting along. Once DeWayne and I started talking again, he would constantly bring up how he would always love us both and how we didn't like each other, causing a rift in order to continue his triangulation. He would say the same things to Amber. Our already fragile relationship started to deteriorate, which was his goal.

Glynn: Was he trying to create a "Sisterwife's" situation?

Ginger: No! He wanted us at odds.

Glynn: That seems more on brand. But did it work? Did you two maintain this tentative friendship? Or...

Ginger: It did work. We soon drifted after the burial of their son. We still communicate for William's sake, but it's very limited. The competition was back on. Besides that, she started back to being a semi-deadbeat, which was always a problem for me. Her behavior deeply affected William and he started rebelling, especially when his dad came back around.

Phoenix: How was William handling the loss of his brother, DeWayne Jr. and your friendship with his mother?

Ginger: I'm sorry. DeWayne Jr. is their biological son. The son who was killed is Amber's son and DeWayne's step-son. William was hurt, of course, but he didn't show it much. He was cool with me and Amber's relationship. He was NOT cool with his dad coming back around. He didn't want him ANYWHERE near me.

Phoenix: I'm confused. Amber had a son before she married DeWayne and they both raised him?

53

Ginger. She had 2 sons before they met, who she abandoned as well.

Phoenix: I see, said the blind man. This relationship was a roller coaster from the start. Now you have your ticket to enjoy the ride.

Glynn: So, just to clarify; Will is NOT DeWayne's biological son?

Ginger: Yes he is. William and DeWayne Jr. are DeWayne and Amber's biological children. Amber had two sons before she met DeWayne. DeWayne had two daughters.

Glynn: Wait-- What?! There are SIX kids involved in this? TOTAL?!

Ginger: Yes, the fucking Brady Bunch! And I'm the empathic "stepmother"!

Glynn: Seems more like you get treated like Alice.

Phoenix: Hahaha! RIGHT.

Ginger: BINGO!!! But in the end, my blessings will come. I just pray for strength to endure this perpetual nightmare and courage to jump off this narcissistic roller coaster...I just can't leave William to these maniacs...so here I sit...STUCK! Pray for me, y'all!

Glynn: I feel for you. Being in a triangulation involving children is rough. It is entrapment. And your wanting to be a healthy alternative to what that child has experienced, is put at odds with every interaction with his/her narc parent(s).

Ginger: It's more than a notion. But, William is graduating in a few months and I'm sending him to college. After he leaves, I wonder what angle DeWayne will come from to remain in my life. I've started noticing his efforts to have a better relationship with Sarah. I'm sure that'll be his next play. We shall see...

Glynn: Well Sarah is an adult, so that won't work well. If I were you I would make sure nothing "needs repair" in your house. That aside, what about DeWayne's daughters? Are they relevant? I have not heard about them in any legitimate context.

Ginger: No! I never established a relationship with them. Their relationship with DeWayne was strained due to his absenteeism when they were growing up. All I know is they had children young and dropped out of high school. But they are nonfactors in regards to our relationship.

Phoenix: The bigger question is what is your plan to keep DeWayne out of your life after William goes off to college?

Ginger: Like I said! Pray for me, y'all!

FOR FUCK'S SAKE

Phoenix: How old is your son? It could be normal toddler behavior.

Glynn: He turned three recently. I don't know if it is typical. It just seems... different. I am trying to be more observant to be sure.

Ginger: Terrible twos AND threes. [laughs]

Phoenix: Well, it sounds like he is still in the egocentrism stage of development. He should grow out of this stage in a few months. Especially if he is around other children his own age.

Glynn: He isn't, though. At least not to my knowledge. I am kept out of the loop with that kind of stuff. If I ask any questions, then they are shut down. Apparently, since I "don't make enough of an effort" I am not privy to knowing anything about my son...

Phoenix: That sucks major balls!

Ginger: What does "don't make enough of an effort" mean? How does that play into you having information about the well-being of your son?

Glynn: It's... It's like I am being made into a deadbeat against my will. I don't understand how to be well and be a father in this kind of situation. Nothing I do is right and I am unable to find proper help.

Phoenix: I keep telling you to file for visitation rights. That is the only way to see your son since Simone will not allow you to see him.

Glynn: That is easy to say. But the reality is far more complicated. Court orders, Child Protective Services, Friends of the Court, etc. I don't have the resources for which to go--

Phoenix: None of those charges were substantiated, right?

Glynn: What charges?

Phoenix: Court orders, Child Protective Services, and Friends of the Court or should I say complaints? But, these issues were not always at play.

Glynn: Court Orders from the Friends of the Court regarding child support. I would have to file for visitation; take that to court. I can't pay for that at the moment and it takes time for it to be filed.

Phoenix: Child support will not prevent you from obtaining visitation rights. I do understand not having the funds.

Glynn: Yeah, I don't understand the process either. This is not what I was anticipating when I found out I was going to be a father. There is more at play, but I can't figure it out. Things don't add up. Everything I try to legally do is halted. It's crazy! I...I don't know. Nothing I plan out makes it to fruition--GAWD, DAMN IT!! It doesn't make any sense. Ah, for fuck's sake...

Ginger: I'm not clear on what's going on. Why can't you file for visitation rights? What's keeping you from fighting this in the courts? Is there something else in play?

Glynn: MONEY! [laughs] I mean it ain't much, but it might as well be a million dollars for me at the moment. [sighs] I am currently out of work, so I don't have much of a case to fight for my child. Nor do I have the means for which to visit my child. Well to clarify, child support is too high. I spend most of my time budgeting what little I have to allocate between living expenses and child support. Before I was laid-off, I was in a pretty good position and in the process of preparing my case. I had spoken with lawyers and other legal professionals and I had been approved for a two-bedroom home. I had furniture on lay-a-way. I had legal documents sent to me in preparation for an appeal. I had all of these things going on and it was all shelved as soon as I lost my job. But that is only part of it. Another part is that due to these financial constraints, Simone is restricting my visitation by demanding that I come to her. She has too much control and she revels in it. Like a tyrannical dictator, she gives orders to everyone around her and demands they comply. If you go against her though, you are severely punished. Her persona is such that she isn't challenged often due to everyone's disinterest to want to get involved; which perplexes me, because they continue to have communication with her. Yet, those that knew me first that know her now, don't talk to me. And when I have been contacted by them, it's as if they are fishing for information under the guise of "checking in" or "being worried". Though, every move I made was being relayed back to her; which in turn, leads me to being chastised by her. Then when I confront those that I confided in, they would be all confused. But wouldn't give me any information saying, "We don't want to get involved." It is a cycle that was cut when I stopped all communication. Now,

I am essentially dealing with this alone. Legal proceedings take money; I have none. Emotional support requires friends; I have few. All I want is to see my son; I am denied that. My options at this point are to fully concede all my dignity and abide by the rules she sets or be in the position I am in currently; isolated, broke, and despondent. I mean, until I "get my shit together" as she put it. You would think I was some drunk, abusive, toxic, drug-addicted, criminal with the way I am being treated.

Phoenix: Wooooooooow! Take a breath, my brother. I am exhausted just listening to all this. Child support is a different matter than visitation and goes through a different case system. I can't understand why the Friends of the Court didn't order visitation at the child support hearing. It doesn't make sense to have a separate hearing. Sometimes the court system can make things so complicated.

Glynn: Well, from what I was told, I can file more than one motion at the same time. But, I have to pay for EACH motion that I file.

Phoenix: Do they give you any Vaseline before they bend you over? That is ridiculous!

Ginger: EXACTLY, Phoenix!

Glynn: [laughs] They prefer sandpaper. It's as if I have to control the optics. I have to be seen making an effort, but I also need to appear to be stable. Then, I have to make it apparent that I am being hindered by Simone. That is difficult because having three kids BEFORE I met her, she is accustomed to dealing with the system in this fashion; not to mention she is given too much power. This is most apparent with my son's health. As you know, my son Noah was born ill. As such, he has been hospitalized almost every month of his existence. But since his birth, Simone has tried--and in some cases been successful--to use her motherhood to manipulate how much information I receive regarding my son's condition. When Noah was born, he was diagnosed with a fairly uncommon disease. We found this out the next day; after most of the medical tests were completed. I was understandably concerned as a father and wanted more information regarding the specifics of the disease. The doctor who told us the results asked me to step outside as I had further questions. Simone was in the hospital bed resting from labor, but interjected every time I asked a question for clarity. The doctor wanted to show me what he was explaining on the computer right outside the hospital room. But when we stepped out to take a look, Simone, in her weakened state, made the effort to get out of bed and shuffle over to the door to chastise me for having the doctor explain things to me instead of her. She exclaimed that she wants me to be involved, yet if I attempt to do so, she shuts it down. Being that Noah is constantly at the hospital at any given moment, it can be overwhelming dealing with her overbearing disposition. She has these wildly inconsiderate expectations that I believe resulted in us being banned from the hospital closest to her home. This forced her to travel to the hospital in the city-- a point she makes everyone aware of when Noah has to be admitted (doctors, nurses, medical administrators, janitors, etc.). Everyone has to know how much of an inconvenience it is for her to be there. If that isn't the worst of it, she proceeds to engage in verbal spats with anyone who doesn't sympathize with her situation. She has had numerous confrontations with medical staff. One time was with the specialist Noah was seeing regarding his condition. She went back and forth with the physician during a routine monthly check-up. When I tried to inquire about anything, as a means to keep things on track, she turned on me. After which, the doctor pulled me into her office and asked, "Do you always let her talk to you like that?" To which I replied, "So you see it too?" She then told me that I need to do something about Simone's attitude as it is not conducive to a healthy emotional environment for Noah; adding that if I didn't do something, then he would treat me the same way. But my response to her was, "How?" Legal matters take time and I can't physically shut her the fuck up when she starts mouthing off. I can sit there and take it. Even if she starts a confrontation in front of everyone and I engage with her, I am the bad guy. And that is just me standing my ground verbally. If I stand there, soft-spoken and calm, then I am a milquetoast bitch-made boy who isn't strong enough to be called a man. So, here we have me fighting the perception of what I am on all ends. Each action I take is being judged as the wrong actions; even the right ones. Yet, honestly? I couldn't give a fourth of a F-U-C-K about all of that. At the end of the day, what matters most is Noah and that he has a well-adjusted family unit. He is going through so much and it pains me to not be there, but be told to fight for him. But don't fight in front of him. Then to be asked to spend time with him, but that ain't enough. Then pay child support, but child support doesn't make me a father. I am expected to be there consistently, but she doesn't want me over her house. She says I can take him, but doesn't want him to leave the house. Life won't cut me a break. I have spent more time with Noah at the hospital than I have with him when he is well. And this is all because of the distance it takes for her to travel; not because she wants me there. Meanwhile, I choose to keep my distance when he is well, for my sanity's sake; all the while regretting EVERY moment missed, as that is time I will never get back. And I wish to GOD that is where it ended. But for every avoided phone call, I am left a voicemail disparaging me as a parent. Or, I am sent text messages disgracing me as a man. But, in an effort to lure me back in for the abuse, I will be sent a picture of Noah laughing and playing as if to say, "This is what you are missing out on." She uses her single motherhood as a means to claim victimhood and portray me as the deadbeat dad. When she never had any genuine emotion invested in me. [voice breaking] I can't fight off all these obstacles and protect Noah. It crushes me to see myself become a ghost before my son's very eyes. .

Ginger: OH...MY...GOD!!! I have so many concerns for you! I'm so sorry that you're experiencing this. WOW! So she has completely taken control of the rearing of your son. I agree with the doctor. Eventually, she'll turn your child against you. It's clear that her plan has been initiated to make you look incompetent, less than, disregarded, and irrelevant. Does your son show any signs of switching up on you? You stated that Simone has other children? How are the relationship(s) with the other father(s) and her other children? Low key, I'm ready to kick her ass, myself!

Glynn: Yes, Simone has three children not including our son. I was under the impression that the relationship between them and their fathers was either poor or nonexistent. I spent a large chunk of time with them. Though, according to her, it didn't mean shit. I don't know what she thinks a father figure consists of, but she would constantly praise me for being an excellent one. Only for her to criticize me for not being better at it; especially after Noah was born. It's like those prior eight years didn't exist, but I was also expected to be her perception of the perfect parent. Her relationship with her kids is that of a monolithic one. Where she stands as the sole provider, emotional supporter, disciplinarian, and decision-maker. She complains about her lot in life, as though she was handed the short end of the stick. But if you offer her any help, she will not accept it. Instead, she suggests the kind of help she would prefer, then kind of persuades you to assuage her. There is no compromise and you only get credit as a means to keep you around. At this point, my perception of her children has been clouded with so many lies and so much manipulation, it is hard to tell what the deal is with them. But I can tell you that we once had a stronger rapport than we do currently. She would attribute that to my insistence to abandon the family motif that I had built up. But, it is more factually accurate to say that I was forced out.

Ginger: WOW!

Glynn: I attended her eldest son, Kenneth's, graduation from high school. His father was supposed to show up, but didn't. Simone then called me to verify that I was coming, stating that Kenny didn't need any further disappointment. Even though, leading up to the event, she constantly tried to uninvite me. Doing everything including refusing to give me tickets, not inviting my parents, and trying to block me from making contact with Kenny. But when the day arrived, it was all, "Where are you?" "Are you here yet?" "Hurry up to the seats!" etc. I have now come to the realization that she was probably just trying to make Kenny's father look bad by having me show up. As if to say, "Glynn is a better father than you. Kenny isn't even his son and he still came to support." Smoke and fucking mirrors, I swear.

Ginger: Yep! Her bit of manipulation and triangulation! Poor her!

Glynn: RIGHT! Like if she is hungry, she will tell you that she hasn't eaten all day and her stomach hurts. So you might suggest grabbing her something to eat, only for her to refuse. But if you don't do it, then she will complain until she goes to bed. So what you are "supposed" to do is take that comment and make it your priority to solve. Find menus, suggest restaurants, ask follow up questions, etc. You need a game plan. I say this, but one of a dozen things can happen to result in her being unsatisfied with the outcome. Even if you accomplished everything you were subliminally conditioned to do, then the restaurant might have fucked up; which happens a lot for some reason. And to that effect, me and her other children had a running joke about how many restaurants we couldn't go to due to claims of "poor service". [sighs] There were many.

Phoenix: Ooh-wee!!!! My head is spinning. How did all this get started? And did you say she had three kids when you met her and that you have been dealing with or dating Simone for eight years?!!!!!!? I don't think I would have lasted that long. Just after three months with Chris, I was planning my escape. [laughs] I saw the writing on the wall and made my plan. I stopped arguing with him and had a nonchalant attitude. When he would leave the house in anger, I ignored his tantrums. I would sing Big Sean:

I don't fuck with you!

You little stupid ass bitch, I ain't fuckin' with you!

You little dumb ass bitch, I ain't fuckin' with you!

I got a million trillion things I'd rather fuckin' do.

Than to be fuckin' with you...

And I really didn't give two fucks about him anymore. I had emotionally withdrawn from Chris. Just looking at him made me physically sick. When he would say, "I'll be back." My response was, "You don't have to." He would tell me he loved me; then ask if I believed him. I would tell him, "No. How can you love me when you don't love yourself?" He would just look at me. I just stopped playing his game. For me, being in a loving healthy relationship shouldn't be this jungle gym of emotions with questions of my self-esteem. I decided that I was good enough - actually better before I met Chris. I begin to ask myself why am I with him? What is he offering that I can't provide for myself? So, I started back doing my nightly Deepak meditation, deep breathing exercises, and using my Himalayan salt rock to center myself. When Chris would raise his voice, I would mimic his actions then say, "Bam, bam, bam," then walk away. I nicknamed us Pebbles and Bam Bam. [laughs] But I had a peace of mind after six months of this process. And it was a process.

Glynn: That is a process that is easier to pull off when Triangulation is limited. It is weird for me because I feel like Simone was more or less telling me the same thing that you said to Chris. I knew I was never what she wanted, but thought I was better suited for her. And this is based on what she told me of her past and showed me of her life. Honestly, I just wanted to fix her. I don't mean like she was a project for me to undertake. But I wanted to show her how to have a healthier relationship. Seems like she was doing everything she could to sabotage it and ruin my reputation in the process. After a while, I felt like a losing contestant on "Flip That Narc"; trying to be valuable while being devalued. Yet, she insisted on having me work for her until she found someone better, even if I had nothing of value to add to her life. I have been there before, so it's not like I didn't recognize the signs. Usually, when a woman tries to put me on retainer, I leave with no qualms. But her having children that I had developed a familial connection with was what made staying worth it. It was like, for every bad moment, there was one where the kids made me feel accepted. It was like they were my safe space while I was there. We were building a healthier relationship than she and I had. But of course, she worked to destroy that too; which was done over time. Like she was waiting for them to get to an age where I could be seen as no longer essential to their development. All while degrading my inability to deal with the stresses she was burying me under. It was virtually impossible to know what she wanted!

Phoenix: Oh my goodness; I felt the same way! Like I was a placeholder until Chris found someone better. Nothing I did was ever good enough. It got to the point that one of his sons told me he felt bad for me. "I don't understand why he treats you like that? He gets mad because he has to pay bills. I told him that is part of being a man with responsibilities." It was like he was used to having women taking care of him. Just because you have a big dick doesn't mean you are God's gift to the world. I mean, please. If you want to be in a relationship, it takes work from both parties.

Glynn: But it also means both parties working for a common goal.

Ginger: Is this real? No WAY we all have the same story. DeWayne hates me! I'm convinced of it. He's always trying to degrade me and I always felt that he only wanted me around because he had no other choice. He had also gotten very comfortable with me and I became more of a habit than someone he actually cared about. But, I figured out what all of this means! We are all PRIMARY sources of SUPPLY for these users. They need supply like we need oxygen and they'll do whatever they need to do to get it.

Phoenix: That part!!!!

Ginger: We can try to make ourselves be less of an object to them, but the truth is, WE'RE not. Honestly, there is no common goal. We are not a team! We are in constant competition. Because they constantly move the goal post, we will NEVER win. Rules are adjusted, midway, to put them ahead...Manipulation, triangulation, gaslighting, and diabolical mindsets are not a part of our playbook! These veterans know the game and they play it very well. The game is designed for us to lose, and we will, EVERY TIME.

Glynn: It feels like you are working for them to accomplish what they want. Like they have life planned out, but you are just a means to an end. If you aren't doing what they want you to do, then you're used for whatever they can get out of you. I shouldn't have gotten so attached. As soon as you feel like you can make a difference in their life, that is when you fucked up. Your idea of healthy is not what they perceive as beneficial. You have to think like they think. And as soon as you do, they will change it. Simone was constantly pushing me away just to pull me back. Once we had a child together, she didn't have to pull often. Now it is expected of me to endure her mistreatment, while knowing that I am disposable.

Phoenix: Everyone in their world is disposable and recyclable. If they can keep you in their constant loop, they will.

Glynn: I am not unfamiliar with that concept. I used to keep some very toxic friends around. I even had an open door policy for women I felt weren't harmful to me. But that was mostly due to me not letting my guard down; especially if they wronged me in the past. I never actively sought out people to repair and reunite with under the banner of "Fuck that person!" Simone is different though. I know for a fact that one of her manipulative tactics is, "yeah, but that was me and him. What's that got to do with you and me?" She likes to isolate me by keeping people on her side or neutral. And she would emphasize that! Like Simone will keep me from seeing my son and my mom knows this; she sees it happening in real-time. But Simone will try to make it so my mom can see my son behind my back. If my mom "chooses" not to play that game, Simone will accuse her of being petty for letting our issues prevent her from seeing her grandson.

Phoenix: I don't even know what to say. It's like we kind of set ourselves up for failure. On one hand, we love the person but we hate them for how they treat us. It's like gambling. You like the rush of winning but losing drives you more to keep playing with the thought of winning "The Houses" money.

Ginger: And ain't gone win shit!!!

Phoenix: You can only hope to break even.

Glynn: I am curious; is it really love? At this point, I feel like it may be L.O.D.E. that is driving this insane emotional investment.

Ginger: It definitely isn't LOVE, but L.O.D.E? What's that?

Glynn: Loneliness, Obsession, Desperation, and Ego.

Phoenix: On who's part? Ginger: Both?

Glynn: Possibly. But, in your case Ginger, I feel it's like that on DeWayne's part by the way he clings to you. In my case, I am not so sure. Like, my continued motivation is that I want good things to come to pass and a healthy well family unit. But, I feel as though I shouldn't attempt that with her because, duh, she ain't safe. But I have been dealing with her for so long, I can't see past her. And trying to adjust to being free of her only has me questioning if there was something that I missed that could have been discussed. And I know that isn't true. We talked about everything twice. And if it wasn't talked about, it is because she didn't want to work on it. I am single now, hence the loneliness. I am convinced I could have done something different or better;

hence the obsession. I am desperate to be with my son. And my ego won't accept failure from all the above.

Ginger: Is the desperation only about your son?

Glynn: Glad you asked me that. The answer is no, it is not. [long pause.]

Phoenix: Well, don't keep us in suspense!

Glynn: [laughs] Ok. Ok. Well, the truth -- and I may have stated this before-- is family. But to elaborate a bit, I was trying to be a stable, reliable, consistent, and a positive presence in Simone and her children's lives. By being pushed out constantly, it makes me want to try harder to show them that I am not a shitty person; as well as support them how I can. And get my son to see me as his father! But it comes at the cost of the detriment of my self-worth.

Ginger: [sighs] We are always trying to prove that we are good enough and they consistently tell us that we are not. Finding fault in others helps them to not focus on their inadequacies. This is why they stay so long in the Devaluation Phase.

Glynn: Something I noticed is how Simone would often try to diminish my intellect because I wasn't accomplished as say... Well, you two. Like, because I don't have accolades or credentials, I am not apt enough to advise her on anything; nor are my thoughts valid. But she can't shut the fuck up about any particular topic. And I am just expected to sit there and listen. Oh, and I am always wrong. And if I come back with verification that I was right, then I am petty for harping on "old shit". It's ok if she does it though. [sighs]

Phoenix: The main issue is they don't love themselves. How can they love another if they don't have self-love? They are constantly looking for reassurance from others to foster their low self-esteem. If it is not supplied, they will seek it out by any means necessary. Even if that means hurting the people or person that gives them unconditional love and admiration.

Glynn: Does vanity count? Because she loves her own image.

Ginger: YES, Sir! Quick history lesson (the teacher in me can't resist). In Greek Mythology, Narcissus (where the term narcissism comes from) was in love with his image. He saw a reflection of himself in a river. Look it up!

Phoenix: Glynn, that is just a cover-up for how they truly feel about themselves. They are really insecure, hence, the need for frequent attention, ego-stroking, and admiration.

Ginger: ABSOLUTELY, Phoenix!

Glynn: [retches] Nope. [dry heaves]. Nuh-unh. It's not in me to shower someone with adulation who craves it. Maybe it's the contrarian in me, but I refuse. Plus, she doesn't deserve it. What is gross is how she will shower herself with praise out of fucking nowhere. Like, she loves her hair right? Mainly because it is all hers; no weave, wigs, etc. But it ain't super impressive. The way she gushes over it, you would think she was Rapunzel. But if ANYONE compliments her on her hair and you weren't present, she will tell you about it. Like you have never seen her head before. Hell, one time when leaving the hospital, she told our three year old son about some random dude admiring her hair. Like, a whole story! I thought she was talking to me (which she probably was), but she was like, "I was talking to Noah." Yeah, ok. Like he gives a fuck about that corny shit.

Ginger: Such low self-esteem! It's so obvious! DeWayne needs that same admiration for things that he does. Depending on what it is, I'll give him some adulation. Sometimes, they need that shit... Sometimes they deserve it. It's harder for me to hate the guy than it is for him to hate me. But, contrary to popular belief, they TOO can be manipulated.

Phoenix: Glynn, you acknowledged that you are a contrarian. Do you think that may be why you two are always at odds with one another? You two are like oil and water.

Glynn: True. I don't like the status quo and don't follow trends. That's where my contrarian nature comes into play. And she is more of a popular person's person. As the old phrase goes, "She is more country and I am more Rock 'N Roll." It's weird because that is how she carries herself, but she likes to claim to be the opposite. Like she is an actual contrarian. She won't allow us to be on the same page. It's like she refuses to have us be equal. And lord knows, if I am making headway at becoming stable or moving up-- Woo, boy!-- The amount of vitriol and animosity she holds toward me could heat a kettle for your afternoon tea.

Phoenix: Sounds like there is some grandiosity going on here.

Glynn: In what way do you mean? You mean with me?

Phoenix: No. The statements about you not being equals and questioning your intelligence. It's as if you are inferior to her. Did you think I was referring to you?

Glynn: A little bit when I mentioned me being a bit contrarian. Questioning the status quo is what I do though. Sometimes, things just seem… off. In a relationship, I like to find out what is best for us. Not aspire to be what other couples are. There were a lot of times she just showed me that she felt deserving of things that she didn't put the work towards. Like all her friends were getting married, so that became a whole thing. There was constant infidelity, but I was just supposed to forget it and move on. But let me have any interaction with someone that she saw as "questionable"? Oh, then *I* was cheating and she knew it. No evidence, just a gut feeling. I was just out fucking everyone for some reason. I was guilty, if not guiltier than her because she wanted me to be. That's it.

Ginger: The projectionist at work…[laughs] But I wanted to touch a little bit on what Phoenix mentioned above: Grandiosity! Another characteristic of the narcissist. They will make themselves bigger than they truly are. They brag about things they don't have and make others look up to them, even when the narcissist is beneath them. It's amazing how they work. DeWayne used to talk about his days as a big-time ATL drug Kingpin, while he's living in his mother's basement. HILARIOUS! He wanted to impress me and others so desperately. After a while, I saw right through it!

Glynn: What is a testament to that is if you have accomplishments, they feel equal to you. But if you don't, then you aren't. Only if you are at a status they have yet to achieve, that they deem superior, will you be able to be heard unequivocally. Even then, they will find enough fault in you to bring you down to their eye level, just so they can ignore you. Or they will tear you down to make you feel bad for what you have accomplished. Hell, it's like the only time Simone ever saw herself beneath me, was when we were fucking.

SEX AS A WEAPON

Ginger: [singing in the kitchen]...*And when we're done...I don't wanna feel my legggssss...and when we're done...I just wanna feel your hands all over me babbyyy...Baby let me be YOUR motivation!!* WHEW!! He put it DOWN last night [scrambling eggs in a nightie]. He knows all my spots and hits them before he makes a move! He uses my weakness for his advantage and I let him...like kryptonite...Y'all know what I mean?

Glynn: You just gonna start singing randomly, huh? Gotta say, I was not expecting that. But to answer your question. No. No, I don't think I know what you mean. Please, if you don't mind, elaborate...

Phoenix: Ginger must have gotten that good, good last night. He got a BITCH sangin'!

Glynn: Yeah, about that...Why are we just now hearing about this?

Ginger: Old news! I'm just reminiscing about how we would have great makeup sex and we'd be back together afterward. So, after a discard, DeWayne would pop up to my house, banging on my door for hours. I would watch him on my security camera. Eventually, I would give in to the begging. Once, it was about 20 degrees outside and he had walked a couple miles. Empathic me let him in, but the bitch in me had him out there, banging. I guess...no, I KNEW the outcome once I opened that door. He had a sexual hold on me as well. You know they use sex as another tool in their narc toolbox! He would go extra hard in the paint to secure his supply. Then, I would be back in it. "Why am I back in it?" I already knew the outcome! Oh, I know! I'm INSANE! Insanity: doing the same thing over and over and over again and expecting a different result. But honestly, I don't expect a different result. But I do expect a different play. The sex was just his way in and my legs were wide open for it...AGAIN!

Glynn: Um, well all right. [laughs] Phoenix? Anything to add?

Phoenix: Well, I was dickmatized after the first time. We spent a Saturday afternoon together just talking and walking at Milliken Lighthouse. We had dinner and decided to stay the night together at a hotel. I showered first. As I got out of the shower, I had an overwhelming feeling come over me. I opened the door to see Chris laying on the bed. I closed the bathroom door and just smiled. I walked out with only my towel on. He then got in the shower as I laid on the king-size bed waiting for him. He opened the door and walked out with stream from the shower hiding him. As he walked closer to me, my body felt weak and excited at the same time. He told me to take off my towel and he looked at my naked body and lowered his body onto mine. We looked into each other's eyes and passionately kissed for what seemed to be 20 minutes. His kisses were hot and wet which made me wet. He began to kiss my neck then slowly kissed and sucked my breast. My body moved in rhythm with each kiss. The touch of his hands gave me goosebumps. We licked and sucked each other for hours. Oh, but when he made me cream, it felt like our bodies became one. When it was all over, we fell asleep in each other's arms. I knew then, I was in for a problem.

Ginger: Oh lawd! I might need a cold shower...[laughs] DeWayne knows he's my weakness. He'll stop begging for forgiveness and say, "Come here, Ginger." I'd go the other way and the chase was on. Once he had me in his grips, I'd melt into him. It's not like he put it down like a porn star. I think it's mostly mental. But it works for him...It works for me, too, but only in that moment. So, Glynn, tell us, is Simone a "sexual goddess?"

Glynn: So we just gon-- Ok. I guess this is happening, then. [laughs] Um. I wouldn't say she is a sexual goddess. More like a seductive succubus; as in she sucks til I bust.

Phoenix: Ha, ha, ha, a succubus! Are you also saying you are a sleeping man?

Glynn: No, no. I was joking. To be honest though, it was as if her body was a sexual theme park. She was very intuitive. It didn't take much. She had a way of getting in my head. There was one time when I came over to watch a movie. I didn't think much of it. I had no expectations but at a certain point, she went upstairs and came back down in a black negligee. I saw her and I forgot all about the movie. She put on a little show before walking over to me and putting her foot on the arm of the couch. She was standing there, in a Captain Morgan pose, blocking the view of the TV at this point. She asked, "You like what you see?" I looked her dead in the eye and said, "Hell yeah!" She was like, "Whatcha gonna do about it?" I got up off the couch and pulled her down, rolled her over, and undressed what little she had on. We had sex

77

on that couch for the duration of that movie. But it didn't stay like that. After a while, shit changed. Sex came up more as a means of control on a moment-to-moment basis. It was used more as a tool than an act of intimacy. Eventually, it was more transactional than emotional.

Ginger: It's funny how they use sex as a weapon against you. I heard that the female narcissist was more diabolical with using sex to get and maintain control...although DeWayne has used it for control purposes as well. We, women, do use sex to get you guys in line [snickering]. When DeWayne was on his bullshit, he couldn't touch me with a 10 ft pole. I learned a few manipulation tactics from him. But then he'd manipulate me right back with "I'm sorrys" and fake epiphanies to get in my panties...And it worked! So technically, he won again! [laughs]

Phoenix: I guess I'm different. I am NOT using sex as a punishment. I loooove it too much to not get it. Besides, angry sex is the best! Shit, smack my ass and tell me I've been bad. Or is that just me? But, Chris, he would hold out if I walked wrong. We went from having sex four to five times a week to maybe once a week. I was sexually deprived and frustrated! He knew I loved to have sex and he used it against me. I began to resent him for it because I knew he was using it to try to control me.

Glynn: See, Simone was... disconnected. Sex wasn't meaningful to her. It was just something to do, but also something that I shouldn't do with anyone else. That rule only applied to me, by the way. She would often accuse me of being with other women. She'd make it seem like the idea of me being with anyone else was just dirty as fuck! When I found out about all the moments of her infidelity, she had little to say. Her logic was that sex was like drinking; not to be taken too seriously, even though serious repercussions could occur from it. Sometimes she would try to use sex to solve issues around her promiscuity. I wouldn't always bite though. No pun intended.

Phoenix: Chris was the same way as Simone. Sex became a task to Chris with little emotion behind the act. I recall one time while we were having sex, he looked into my eyes and said, "Really Phoenix, you can stop making all that noise." He had gotten cold and seemed uninterested in making love. We were now FUCKING. There were no emotions or sensuality. At times, I felt like a rape victim. Or Celie from The Color Purple. "I just lay there and let Mister do his business." You know? Just lay here and take it. It will be over soon. I was also accused of cheating. Really? I'm with you damn near 24/7, the dick is AMAZING. There was no need to cheat. But, he could text women all hours of the day and night. I think I told y'all his phone was another appendage. He didn't want me to look at, touch, and most definitely not answer his phone. He would even leave the room to talk. But I could always hear his side of the conversation.

Glynn: All right, I can relate to the phone thing. I am guilty for being on my phone a lot or even having a close eye on it. That stems from her going through it on a couple of occasions and confronting me, though. It was like she was looking for dirt to justify doing dirt. Thing is, she didn't find anything that was extra. Not like the shameless debauchery that kept spilling out of her life. Somehow, whatever mild things she saw was comparable to her hedonistic hotline. I couldn't make sense of it.

Phoenix: I never kept my phone from him or left the room to take a call. I mean, I had nothing to hide. Even if a male called me, he could have answered the phone. But he was jealous. He told me he didn't like me talking to other men. I asked him if he realized I was very social and had A LOT of male associates. Glynn, he was jealous of you too! After the company picnic, he told me I shouldn't talk to YOU. I just flat out told him that was not going to happen. That I had friends before I met him and I will continue to have friends with or without him. I have never been the type to be controlled.

Glynn: Yo!! I remember that picnic. I was there with Simone's youngest kids at the time. I was wholly preoccupied and we barely spoke that day! If anything, of the other male co-workers there, I was the safest for you to talk to, being that I was wrapped up in my own shit. [laughs]

Ginger: OMG! This is hilarious. DeWayne and I split for a year after he was caught cheating. After about 9 months, I slept with someone else. When we rekindled, we talked about things and I told him about it. He had a conniption. Sir, you were in a whole relationship for months with your ex-wife. WHAT THE FUCK?

Phoenix: So, you and DeWayne separated for nine months and you let him back in? What in the world were you thinking? Or, was your vajayjay doing the thinking? Where were you when you allowed this to happen? Please don't tell me he popped up again at your house.

Ginger: Yep! As I said earlier, I was "in control" when he hoovered me at my sister's house and he ended up eating my pussy. We would have different blowouts, big ones, because he loves pushing limits, and I would discontinue the relationship. He would show up at my house then too and talk his way back into my thongs. Popping up at my house is his signature move.

Phoenix: I don't do pop-ups. If Chris didn't call first, he would just stand on the porch, ringing the doorbell as I watched through the peephole. But, there was this one time he called to ask if he could pick up some clothes. At this point, we had already broken up and he moved out of the house. When I opened the door, there was an instant sexual attraction on both of our parts. Our eyes locked, we kissed, and then he picked me up and carried me to the dining room table. He lifted my dress and thrust inside of me. It was glooooorious! No, wait, actually he was only inside me for under a minute. The next day I felt a little itchy. So, I made an appointment with my OBGYN. Sure enough, I had chlamydia. That funky BASTARD! The disadvantage of not using a condom. Luckily it was something that was curable.

Ginger: GIRL! Speaking of STDs. We were on a brief 3-week break. I had HAD it, again. Once he came back, we had awesome sex and a few days later, my shit was itching like mad. I wanted to take a Brillo pad to it. I confronted him. He was humble as fuck. I wasn't ready for his response. I thought he would gaslight me and accuse me of sleeping with someone. He didn't. But guess what this muthaphukka did? He PRAYED for me...for us! "Dear Lord, we humbly come to you in this, our time of need, to pray that Ginger doesn't have a sexually transmitted disease. We have been through so much together and we don't need a sexually transmitted disease. Please, if Ginger is infected, cure her totally and completely! We ask this in your holy authentic name, Jesus! Amen." I almost died right there. How are you going to pray for me after YOU infected me? The narcissist knows NO BOUNDS! Right then, I KNEW he had something and had infected me. I confronted him again, especially after my urine smelled like horse shit. He finally came "clean"... said he got his dick sucked! REALLY!!! REALLY!!! That's what you're going with? You know I INSTANTLY jumped on Google and found out that many STDS can be transmitted orally. Dude, if she gave you an STD from oral sex and it got my pussy smelling like shaving cream and fish eggs, you should have smelled that bitch coming! SMDH!! I couldn't prove it, but I am STILL sure that he fucked…RAW! Ugh!!!

Glynn: What random hobo did he meet at the Boxcar Convention? You know what? NOPE!! Fuck that! Wait, scratch that-- DON'T FUCK THAT!!

Phoenix: I'm still stuck on the shaving cream and fish eggs. I didn't even tell Chris because I didn't want to hear his lies. I had not been with anyone but him, so I knew where I contracted the STD.

Ginger: I thought I would be accused, but he owned it. I knew where mine came from, too. What's hilarious is how he love-bombed me for months behind it. I got everything I wanted and more. If I breathed heavy, he was checking on me. This clown started bringing me tea and cooking for me. He cleaned my house from top to bottom. He would peck me on the forehead every day and say the sweetest things. I would look at him in total disgust and think to myself: You dirty community dick having ass bastard! You nasty muthaphukka! Why the fuck am I infected, you nasty fuck! Personally, I think he fucked raw with some hooker whore he paid…For a very long time, I suggested that he find some other pussy to fuck because the GINGERBREAD HOUSE was boarded up!

Phoenix: What are you talking about, Glynn?

Glynn: Nothing. I just got heated for a second because I had a similar experience. But let me tell you how this chick tried to gaslight me with this shit. So, Simone hits me up one day-- by this time we weren't even having sex enough for it to be anything super significant. But still, I allowed it to happen as a means to be closer to her. I thought it was more important than just a superficial physical activity. Anyway, she called me and asked if I was around anyone at the moment. I said, "Naw. Why?" I was under the impression she wanted me to come through for some late-night loving. But what she actually called to tell me was that I should get tested because she thinks I gave her something. I was like, "Excuse me, what?" I told her that wasn't possible because we used condoms. Then I asked if she had been having unprotected sex with someone else?" She got quiet. I ask,"Who was it?" She said, "None of your business." I asked if I knew him. She said, "No." I was heated, of course. But whatever. I got tested and it came back negative. I showed her the results and she called this random mofo in front of me and said, "Yeah, Glynn just got his test results back and they were negative. So that means you gave me this shit." I was PISSED!! I was like, "Yo!! Who the fuck is that on the phone that knows me?" I mean, if I don't know the dude, how are we on a first-name basis? After the most inflammatory argument, she tells me it was Kenny's dad, Ken, Sr. Then she had the nerve to tell me that I once said I would be more understanding if I found out about her fucking one of her baby's daddies. Which I did but, the fuck?

Phoenix: You mean to tell me she used your words against you to justify her cheating? Classic!

Ginger: CLASSIC!!!

Glynn: I know, right? But for fuck's sake, that didn't excuse the situation. Not only did I know that dude, she frequently told me that he wasn't shit. Earlier that year, she had been all up in arms because he didn't attend Kenny's high school graduation. But, she still managed to pre-plan a trip to "bust it open" for this dude while having me "babysit" my son for a weekend? [scoffs] After that shit, she got no more dick from me. But she insisted she could get it from me at any time. Up to that point, she was kind of right.

Phoenix: Man, Simone has major balls! Honestly though, when Chris first tried to pull away from me sexually, I felt he thought I was no longer attractive. It really wreaked havoc on my self-esteem. I would cry while laying next to him when he didn't touch me or refused my sexual advances. We no longer held each other while we slept. There was this one day after we had not been getting along that he asked me if I wanted to take a walk by the water. I was so excited that he initiated an outing and it was my favorite thing to do. But when we got two blocks from the house, he got a text message and immediately started an argument. Needless to say, we did not go on our outing and he left the house for hours.

Glynn: Is that so? Doesn't that lack of intimacy give sex diminishing returns?

Phoenix: It really does. The next time he called me to tell me he was horny and asked if he could come over, I told him how I felt. "No, the last time was only a minute and the reward was not worth my time. I'm good." He was like..."WHAT?" I explained to him that I was not sexually satisfied and no longer sexually attracted to him. For me, the relationship was emotionally dead. All the feelings I had for this man had dissipated. I began thinking and wondering why I was with him. I mean, he couldn't keep a job, he didn't have a car, he had three children (that I knew of) by three different women, and a temper that was out of this world. Did I tell y'all he was fired from a job because he literally lifted up one of his co-works above his head and was about to throw him? That shit was bananas! There was a time I would have followed Chris to the end of the earth. But now, I have chosen to love myself over him. I replayed our relationship in my head over and over and over again. I realized he was not the kind of man I wanted nor needed in my life. He is not my soulmate. My heart was no longer heavy and my shoulders felt lighter. [exhaling] Ahh, I can breathe.

Glynn: I am very glad that you were able to attain that freedom. Honestly, it sounds like you broke the spell. Self-love is very important. The one thing they will relish in is all your love going directly to them. Simone would get jealous of anyone who had my attention. Everyone around me was telling me I loved her when in reality, I was still figuring that out. By the time I finally came to the conclusion that I did love her, all I got was I-told-you-so's. But it was undeserving because it was an incorrect assumption from the start. I was forced into loving her. I was abused mentally, emotionally, and made to feel inferior, as well as alone. All the while, Simone would present herself to me and others, as the best thing for me. Meanwhile, I was rejecting her internally but accepting her physically. I desperately wanted every sexual encounter to hold the emotional weight of epiphanous passion. Ugh...See, this is where it gets weird for me. I tried to use it as a means to be closer to her. I thought it was more than just a physical activity. I was being manipulated into becoming attached to her physically. I often broke the hold her "snatch" had on me. But then she would find a way to get me back over there or pop up to my house or show up to my work; each time, solidifying her presence in my life. I went into a relationship with her with a decent amount of mirth and self assurance. But as of late, I feel drained of anything that resembles a positive feeling. At least when we were having sex, there was this orgasm of hope, we could work out our differences attached to the activity. Without the sex, I am only left with constant beratement and put-downs. I am finally getting to a place where my self-worth isn't dependent upon her acceptance of me. And seeing or hearing this has her fuming.

Ginger: Hmmm! I guess I may have a different outlook on my relationship with DeWayne. I was never really "in love" with him. He had become a part of my routine. Because of my insecurities with the move and my empathy for William being abandoned by his mother, I stayed. DeWayne became more of a convenience. I tolerated him, probably for my own reasons. I did care for him and I was very sexually attracted to him, but he was never my soulmate. I tried to force love, but I got nothing. People would also say that I needed to admit that I was in love with him. I would go over it in my mind. I would look for reasons why I was in love. I would "admit" that I did love him, but I never FELT it. At times, I would enjoy him...enjoy our time together...Have fun with him. But that feeling never lasted for more than a few days and I would be back in the reality that this person wasn't the one. I had convinced myself that I really wasn't ready for a serious relationship with anyone, so I'd deal with him until I was. I am still not interested. I now know that my psychological abuse at the hands of the many many narcissists that I've been involved with has caused me to swear off the idea of marriage. I assumed I would be a serial dater because, after month 3, I'm over it!

Phoenix: The 90-day rule! I love it and use it.

Glynn: The fucked up part is I saw Simone as greater than, but needing refinement. She apparently always saw me as inferior. Like I was only good enough as a stand-in dad for her kids. Something that I hate is that this confession of feelings comes off as weak. Based on everything she ever told me, that is. If she ever heard me speak this way, she would castrate me. Her opinion of me still holds weight in certain aspects. This is the effects of her cerebral conditioning, I know. But-- (exhales deeply)...Damn it...

Phoenix: Why do we put up with all this?!!! I mean, we know our worth and what we bring to a relationship. Our confidence is high or at least at some level of normal. But, there is something about these individuals that make us weak--No, empathic to their plight. Like you said before, Glynn, at some level we want to fix them or be that supportive person they have been missing all their lives. Maybe that is the part we share in common? If so, that is messed up on our part. The need to be needed. The need to be loved. Or, is it that **we** are co-dependent?

Ginger: I have always been "Captain Save-a-hoe." I think I look for broken people to fix. I don't know why. Maybe it's because of our empathy or our own narcissistic need for accolades. Or, as you stated Phoenix, our need to be needed and/or loved. For me, I think I need to have a purpose. I need to positively impact lives. For my relationship with DeWayne, I guess I did want to mold him into my King. However, after the infamous month 3, his mask slipped and reality kicked in. Nope, he isn't Mr. Right, but he is Mr. Right Now and I have needs that he fulfills. So there I stayed...And here I sit...9 years later...Here I SIT!

CULT OF THE NORTH NARC

Phoenix: It is amazing how people can willingly and unwillingly be manipulated into being a supporting actor in the narcissist's stage play. Especially the people closest to you. But I was lucky. I did not introduce Chris to all of my friends. He only met the ones that I knew would have my back; if needed. I was skeptical in the beginning because Chris wanted to move the relationship along faster than we had discussed. He wanted to meet my mother and was calling her "mommy" before he ever met her. My antennas were up like a cockroach. I made sure we only spent time with his family and friends so I could get to know him better before we engaged with mine. I was not going to supply him with any flying monkeys from my circle.

Glynn: I love that approach! Keep them at bay until you get a better feel for them. What is crazy is how people nowadays try to claim that is wasting time. But there is nothing wrong with taking things slow. I tried to do that. In the case of Chris and DeWayne, they were good actors. But Simone, on the other hand, had ambitions to direct. And the lengths she would go to accomplish this were elaborate and seemingly innocent. Going back a bit to the surprise party, I am not a fan of surprises or anything of the like. Simone knew this and threw one anyway. I met her with my homeboys Tre and Mac, so she knew them already. But, I introduced her to a couple of my other close friends and she did the rest. Because she is attractive, they entertained her presence more than they should. She then used them in a ploy to gather everyone I knew to organize this event. She paid for it and included them in the planning. On the surface, of course, this looked harmless. With everyone getting together in celebration of me, right? Only, I don't like that kind of attention. And once I arrived, everyone there yelled, "Surprise!" I was under the impression that my childhood friends had planned and thrown this party for me. And praised them for remembering my birthday. But, they all let me know it wasn't their idea. Not at all. It was the woman walking up the walkway, fashionably late-- how convenient? From that point, it was The Simone Show. Starring Simone, written by Simone, produced by Simone, and directed by Simone. I was obligated to introduce her to people I was not quite ready for her to know (if at all really) and listen to them gush over her--a veritable stranger. Even my parents who did not know her all that well. She had recruited 75% of my closest compatriots to her cause. And 95% of them were male.

Ginger: The Flying Monkey approach is one used by the narcissist to continue their control over you through other people. If you guys ever watched the Wizard of Oz, the flying monkeys were valuable tools to the wicked witch. She'd send them out to do her dirty work and watch from afar in glorified satisfaction. What was funny was most of them hated her, but were under her spell. Hence, Simone, Chris, and Dewayne. Their family and friends… our family and friends…are used to their advantage as flying monkeys to "GO, MY PRETTIES" and spread dirt or find out information. Everyone is usable; DeWayne used my sister, mother, Sarah, William, and anyone else to either get a message to me (directly or indirectly) or give a message to me. William was his favorite flying monkey. For example, he'd have him call me to see if I cooked. Of course, I wouldn't say no to William. They'd show up an hour later and I'd be back in his grips after his opening and closing arguments. He'd also use my family members. Since he lived so close to my sister, he'd run to her after an argument. He'd plead his case. He'd even use an argument that I might have had with my sister to bolster his point. My sister, being able to see through his bullshit, would stop him in his tracks when he would say, "You know how your sister is. Remember when you two had that disagreement?" She'd cut him off and say, "You're not me and this ain't us!" But, she'd let him finish his story. Then, she'd tell me all about it. Once we realized that he was employing the flying monkey tactic, we decided NOT to ask or tell anything about DeWayne. If I slipped up and asked, she would say, "We're not entertaining the flying monkey!" I mean, I have so many examples of how he used others to get to me. Most were unwilling/unknowing participants, but his SISTER? She stayed ready with her narcissistic ass!

Glynn: Wait--so he has a Narc sister, too?

Ginger: Yes. His mother was the head narc who raised four narcissistic children! When I go back to get my Doctorate in Psychology, these nuts will be my case study. I AM NOT KIDDING! The father is so intertwined that he's picked up many traits from his 50+ years of narcissistic abuse, so I've thrown his ass in the fray, too! It's so amazing to me that I am REALLY considering going back.

Glynn: Yeah, that is something that is never really stated often enough. You can have people's behavior imprinted onto you the longer you interact with them. Narcissists have a way of permeating their personality traits onto those they communicate with until those people come around to the narcissistic way of thinking. It is surreptitious in nature as it is based on its own logic. That being that, as an adult, you can't be persuaded or influenced. Even though any cult survivor would say different. The Cult of the North Narc is one that enlists others by warping the perceptions of right and wrong, causing you to abandon rationale in favor of self-indulgent behavior. The head narc will transform you by catering to the ideals of your inner narc. By doing so, this causes the "new narc" to enable the head narc by reinforcing that behavior based on the indoctrination that occured. Add a flair for emotional relatability and the ability to out talk anyone, not to mention a pension for petty conflict, and you have a completely overbearing persona that takes a tremendous will to combat. The primary purpose of those who are inducted in The Cult of the North Narc is that you ALWAYS look up to the head narc. For he/she is the wisest, most attractive, most mature, most astute person you have ever met. And you are compelled to follow them, for they bring out in you what you see in them. And what that is, is behavior free from judgment and devoid of liability.

Phoenix: Please, I only had Chris' mother's number and he had my mother's number. His nephew and his half brother were the only flying monkeys in our saga. But it was that one time with the dog. For the most part, he had no allies as his family and friends knew he was a liar. Hell, they are the ones who told me to leave him alone. Chris even tried to recruit me as one of his flying monkeys. He would tell a lie, then ask, "Ain't that right P?" I would look at him and ask, "Do you want me to tell the truth?" The answer was always, "Never mind." After the person hung up the phone or left the room, he would say, "You are never on my side." My response was, "Why are you always lying? That is not a good look. Besides, how can anyone trust you when you are always lying or embellishing the truth?" He would smile, give me a hug, and kiss my forehead.

Glynn: I hate that! Simone often said she wanted a man that would support her, even if she is wrong. And there were many examples of that. I would always observe and try to assess the situation calmly from a rational stance. But unlike Chris, when I didn't support her lies or stayed quiet during her public tantrums, she would turn on me. As a matter of fact, she turned on anyone that would not IMMEDIATELY side with her. This included her children. We went for pizza once, and the pizzeria quoted her the wrong price over the phone. When we arrived, she was pissed. She was asking for managers and the like. I asked to see a menu to understand why there was confusion or what have you. Seemed like a simple slip up that could have been resolved with us just canceling the order and walking out if it was that upsetting. But because Kenny and I placed orders also (and were ok with the price), she decided to turn all of her anger on us. She first slung some profanity at her young daughter, Lisa, once we were outside the restaurant. Then when I checked her on that, she went ALL the way in on me; no warning, no filter, no grease. And when Kenny looked at her with the "WTF" face--the same one that everyone outside that busy Saturday night had, by the way—she started in on him also. Then blamed me for pulling him into "our argument." Simone is completely unselfaware and refuses to be held accountable for her behavior. I wish to GOD I was offered a smile, hug, and kiss after not taking her side. But alas, I got court-martialed when I draft dodged or defected from any of her "wars".

Phoenix: See, that is some bullshit! They have no idea how they psychologically abuse their children when they do this. The children are always unwilling participants. They are caught between loving the parent and resenting the parent's behavior.

Glynn: Exactly!! Then, when they get older, they either choose people that are akin to their parents--which perpetuates that psychological abuse, but is familiar--or opt into severing all interaction with them. Thing is, from what I am observing, the amount of control that Simone asserts over all of her children may not allow for them to escape. Even when they transition into adulthood.

Phoenix: This is how narcissists are created. For the most part, it is a learned behavior from social and environmental influences by the primary caregiver.

Ginger: I started limiting interactions with DeWayne's family and eventually, he stopped talking to them. He hated his mother because they were the same narc, so they bumped heads often. DeWayne was, for lack of a better word, a loser. He had his own company that brought in about $1,000 a month. He was gifted with his father's car and he lived in their basement (don't judge me) [laughs]. He owned nothing but hospital bills and a low credit score. No one respected him. His siblings made jokes; especially his sister, who was also the same narcissist. Everyone feared her, including his mother. So, eventually, they stopped talking. His sister, Pauline, would call me to get information on our relationship to share with the family. Depending on how pissed I was with him, I would give her some tea (he hated them in his business). Pauline was also cool with Amber, so I'd let her flying monkey ass run-tell-that and pretend I was none the wiser. In these instances, the flying monkey wasn't working for DeWayne. Or so I thought. Until DeWayne would make a comment, essentially letting me know that he knew. I'll never forget how Pauline was so intentional on getting information to me about DeWayne and Amber's relationship after we broke up. Pauline and I were Facebook friends. After our breakup, DeWayne and Amber were in "Honeymoon" bliss. The family got together for his birthday, videotaped it, and put it on Facebook. Even the sister-in-law was in on the shenanigans. We weren't Facebook friends, but she made sure to make her birthday video public and tagged Pauline. Then a couple months later, the family got together to take Christmas photos. Pauline made sure to post those, too, knowing that I'd see them. On DeWayne and Amber's picture with their sons, she made sure to label it, "DeWayne and his family." For the new year, I decided to be done with the ignorance and blocked them all. Later, while talking with Amber, I brought it up and told her that I knew it was done on purpose. She confirmed that it was. I didn't understand why because I had never done anything to any of them. But because I stayed to myself and because I was cool with the other outcast sister-in-law, I became the enemy to the already fragile narcissistic sister. Her claws were out and she was ready for a fight with me, someone she barely knew. Only after we reconciled and Amber left DeWayne did she try to "friend" me to get information. All of a sudden, Amber was the enemy when talking to me. I'm sure I was the enemy when talking to Amber. Pauline would make snide comments to me like, "My brother will eventually get himself together. For the right woman, he's going to make big moves," or "He'd do anything for Amber. He was working hard when he was with her. I just don't understand how he just loves her so much." I would laugh because I knew she was being deliberately malignant and that her comments were not true at all. DeWayne is a narcissist. He loves DeWayne [laughs]. These people are diabolical in nature. Sick and twisted… Sneaky, cunning, and conniving. The flying monkey was a spy, in essence--a deliverer of news--a dog carrying and delivering bones. Many are unaware of their role while others are complicit. They're dangerous! We all should beware!

Phoenix: And when the flying monkeys are not compliant, the narc will become the "Good Samaritan." Chris played this role to a tee! Chris would do little chores for my mother to gain her trust. Like, one day she called me to do something. Oh! Paint her bathroom. Chris jumped on this like Spiderman. She thought he was so great. Not knowing he told all his family and friends that he did this for her. He praised his efforts and expressed how much she needed him. I wanted to hurl.

Glynn: [laughs] Just your friendly neighborhood Narcissist, at your service.

Phoenix: [laughing and holding stomach] Instead of slinging spider webs, they sling webs of lies!

Glynn: I was gonna say bullshit. But, yeah same thing. [laughs]

Ginger: Honeyyyy! That Good Samaritan is what convinced me to move! Damn, they're good!

Phoenix: Right! And like a fly caught in their web, we struggle to break free only to become more intertwined.

Glynn: The Good Samaritan is the perfect name for that particular behavior they engage in. It is definitely meant to paint them in a helpful, gracious, and selfless light. I always find it funny because it is usually insistent. Like it isn't a favor or helping hand that doesn't come up again and again if you were to go silent on a Narc. Every gift, activity, and/or "good natured" gesture must be recognized, damn near constantly. Or it isn't appreciated. I think it is those instances where people start to see what's going on and begin to distance themselves from the friendship. I would see this happen to Simone often and she would guilt those she "helped" into remaining friends with her. All the while continuing to use them to enable her. But it is a cycle that is dependent on having empathy. If you cannot feel sorry for her or obligated to repay her, then her attempts fail. This will result in her punishing you by shunning until she needs to use you for whatever reason. Then, she will attempt to work it out by way of an "olive branch." Usually this will be a gift of some kind, holding some significance but lacking any real substance.

Ginger: [laughs] Let me tell you about DeWayne's Good Samaritan ass. He would see someone broken down on the side of the road and had to stop, no matter what. Since he was a jack of all trades, he could fix anything. One day, a young lady was stuck on the side of the road with both front tires turned inward. The axle was clearly broken. I laughed when he told me to pull over. There was NOTHING he could do to help her. I pulled over and sat in the car, mad at my time being wasted. About 10 minutes later, she was driving down the road and DeWayne was getting back in the car, feeling accomplished and begging for accolades. EVERYTHING he did was for acknowledgment and accolades. He'd shovel all of the neighbors' snow, sacrifice his own needs to help out to show how great of a person he was. Sacrifice others around him to show strangers that he was a good guy. It seemed genuine until you got to know him. I'll never forget the power outage in the summer of 2012. He was the only person on the block with a generator. It was about 105 degrees outside. DeWayne hooked up the generator between his house and my sister's, who was out of town. She had just bought a freezer full of meat, so we needed to stay powered up. After everything was situated, I went back to my apartment for a while (I had power). When I came back, DeWayne and the generator were gone. I looked around and saw him down the street with extension cords coming from a couple of houses. DeWayne was going up and down the street, allowing neighbors to use the generator while his 70+ year-old parents suffered in 100+ degree weather with no AC. And ALL of the food in my sister's freezer perished. But, DeWayne was the savior for those on the block and they praised his name. I think he may have busted a nut that day.

Glynn and Phoenix [laughing hysterically]

Glynn: Well, at least we know what kind of foreplay he is into.

Ginger: [laughing] Right!

Phoenix: Girl, that is too funny. And speaking of gifts...Chris and I had gone to a gas station to get me something. I gave him $20.00 for the stuff. He came out with my stuff, some stuff for him, and a rose for me. He said, "Here baby, I brought you a rose." I was thinking, NINJA, I bought me a rose. It was my money. Oh, to piggyback on what you said, Glynn, Chris was Johnny-on-the-spot when someone called for a favor. He would give rides (in my car), be a confidant--only to tell their business, use it against them at a later date--or talk about how he was better than the person he helped.

Glynn: Holy shit in a church pew! That is EXACTLY what I think Simone was doing. She would often brag about being the point of contact for her friend's secrets. Like she was the only person they could open up to willingly. But I always felt like she was blackmailing them with information. There were a couple of times where people told me something, only for her to confront them (individually) and have them recant. It always made me think, *What the fuck do you have on these people?*

Ginger: [laughs] Phoenix, I think we may have been dating the same guy. DeWayne, TOO, would offer people rides in my damn car [Shaking my head, followed by a sharp exhale]. This broke fool would even talk about my "raggedy" car until I told him that we could ride on his Nike's. He stopped making negative comments about it after that. Anyway, he would offer my tutorial services or ask me to write recommendations, but sign his name or brag about how good I was with writing to others, me being an extension of him and all. I swear it was never a dull moment in Narcland.

Phoenix: Oh my God, that fool used to do that too! Chris wanted me to write his business plan after he told me how he had written one for his last business in Florida. I was like, get the fuck out of here, dude. You write your own business plan since you are so smart. Needless to say, it never got written. He would also tell his family how smart I was and that I'm a future doctor. Like he was an extension of me and my accomplishments were his. Dude, I wanted to slap the shit out of him. You ain't never done nothing with your life but cause chaos. But he would recant his words by saying, "You ain't smarter than me" or "I can't believe you did something that stupid."

Ginger: This is all so amazing. Everything these fools do is for people to say how great they are. Their low self-esteem, self-image, and self-worth are all wrapped up in what others think. They manipulate everything in their lives just to be a fraction of a decent human being. They find fault in others and use it to build themselves up. Chris' statements were devaluing you in order to make himself feel superior! Simone is constantly emasculating you to make herself seem like the more competent parent. DeWayne can eat shit and die. These maggots go above and beyond to show they're worthy. They perpetuate fraudulence to get attention. They hate who they are and use gaslighting to alter their diminished reality. It's truly sad that these people are this miserable and they cause so much strife. But as they say, HURT PEOPLE HURT PEOPLE! These parasites are seriously, psychologically damaged and hurt!

Glynn: A narc's pain is non-existent. At least, that is the idea I always got from Simone. She wanted to appear so strong at all times. Weakness was something that others had the dissatisfaction of having. And in almost every instance, she would "flex" her strength, while simultaneously putting me down. You are wholly right, Ginger. They *are* hurt people, but you can't know that. You are never supposed to know that.

Phoenix: It's like your own thoughts and what you see with your own eyes are not real. You can be watching tv--the same show mind you--and a character is drinking water out of a clear glass and they will tell you the character is drinking coffee out of a mug. In other words, DON'T BELIEVE YOUR LYING EYES.

Ginger: In a nutshell!

Glynn: How they are perceived is paramount. If it is not a shared belief, then it is uncommon. Common belief is whatever they tell you *they* believe. And it is tantamount that they convince everyone of that. Logic, ethics, and morality are only valuable to those who have a genuine understanding of it; people whose compassion isn't artificial and used in ploys to receive praise. That behavior keeps those around them blind to the true nature of the narcissists. But it also employs those who would otherwise reject their true nature. What often irritates me is how people refute what is true in favor of the presentation of the narcissistic reality. Once an acceptable perception has been established, they then work to have it validate all of their actions going forward.

This means that all of the terrible acts and self-indulgent behaviour is justified as it is retaliation for those that wronged *them*. They are not the catalyst, merely a casualty of the confusion caused by others. As such, they don't receive any condemnation. Rather, they expect and often receive sympathy for their "plight." It was easy for Simone to rally those under her banner using "single motherhood" as a great unifier. If she used anything to help others--gas, money, time, favors, etc.--whether she insisted or not, you were compelled to feel indebted to her. This is because it meant she had to divert resources from her children in order to service those whom she helped, right? This tactic is dependent on you making that assumption. There were moments that I would turn down her assistance, only for her to belittle me for not taking her up on the offer. And if I did, then she would exclaim how I was using her...ugh!! Others are manipulated simply by misdirection or flat out lies. The misdirection is basically double talk, nitpicking, or omission of context. Doing this will weaken any argument made against a narc. Thus, strengthening their appearance to followers even in their absence. If none of that works, then they'll just embellish, exaggerate, or lie. Anyone is susceptible to their deception, but recruitment is dependent on a person's rejection of truth in favor of the narc's narrative.

Ginger: It's not a rejection of the truth, per se, but a manipulation of it. I mean, look at how cults operate. People can see one thing but believe another. Mental games, gaslighting, future faking, etc. are examples of manipulative tactics that work. People often experience cognitive dissonance when dealing with these people. It's not a pleasant experience.

Phoenix: Maaaaaaannn, all I know is this shit is one big headache! With Chris, his family and friends would discuss what a big shot he was. I remember sitting on his cousin, Monique's, porch as she described him getting out of some fancy car with his dreads swinging down his back. According to her, he was dressed in labels from head to toe. Like that was supposed to impress me. She was like, "Girl, he had money! He brought liquor and food to put on the grill. We were royalty that day!" Chris saw me looking at him from the corner of my eye as Monique told his story. He had a slight smirk on his face. But, he saw that I was not impressed as I had a disapproving look on my face. He gestured to Monique to stop by shaking his head. But she kept going on for about 15 more minutes of tales from Chris' past and the women he would bring to her house. Chris was turning red in the face and was ready to go. But not before Monique invited me to a girls' night out party she was having over the weekend. I told her that I would come if I was not too busy with school work. When Chris and I got in the car, he reassured me that that was his past and he wanted a different life with me. He also told me it was not a good idea for me to attend the girls' night out. He said it was a freak party for women, as Monique was into women. I had already made up my mind that I was not attending the party, but Chris' comment made me suspicious. Not of her but of Chris. Something deep down inside my soul felt that another woman he was seeing would be at this party and he did not want our paths to cross. I did not respond to Chris' comment. I just looked at him, turned my head, and looked out the window. And guess what! That was the last time I went to Monique's house.

Ginger: WOW! My nosy ass would have gone. [laughs]

Phoenix: Girl, I didn't even care at that point. I had emotionally distanced myself from him. I was hoping he had someone else so he would get the HELL away from me. Every time I looked at his face, my face would ever so slightly frown. Besides, she had already given away that he was seeing someone else. That same day, this car pulled up in front of Monique's house as she, her husband, three neighbors, Chris and I were on the porch. Chris walked to the car and they ALL looked at me at the same time. I watched Chris as he spoke to this woman. She did not stay very long. But Monique's husband went to the car and gave her a little plastic baggie. She took it and drove off. Monique then said how she liked me over all the women Chris brought to her house. She told him he needs to stay with me. I was thinking, "Bitch, I don't want his ass!"

Ginger: Flying Monkeys!! [laughs] She was on her job that day. "Ma'am, please don't blow smoke up my ass. Chris is a whole loser. I'm good!"

Phoenix: Right!

Ginger: I remember DeWayne's narc ass mother told me that she really liked me while talking about Amber like a dog. His mother said, "Well if Pauline (her narc daughter) liked me, she did too." These two demons worked together on their bullshit. I SWEAR it's nothing worse than a female narc times two. Glynn, I don't know how you deal with that diabolically-possessed nut job. The narc duo that my spirit had to contend with exhausted me to no end. I wouldn't even invite them to my house. His sister's son would stay over some nights with William, so Pauline had been there. The mother has never seen the inside of my home. I don't think there's enough sage in Atlanta to smudge her demonic spirit out. I have enough issues with keeping her son at bay. I remember praying, smudging my home, and pouring salt around my entryway. DeWayne came to the door. He asked why it was salt down. I told him it was to keep negative spirits out. He smirked, giggled a bit, and stepped his ass right over my threshold. I just shook my head! Hell, I probably needed a seance.

Glynn: Honestly, I would suggest an exorcist. But good luck getting them into a church. [laughs]

Ginger: Ohhhhh, let me tell you how DeWayne used to pray every night before bed. Hahahahahaha! They use religion, too! EVERY SINGLE NIGHT! For years, he would not go to sleep until he read a scripture. I would look at him in amazement. Finally, I said to him, during a heated exchange, "Sir, do you know who ELSE knows that Bible backward and forward??? LUCIFER!" His evil ass walked away!

Glynn: [laughs] Simone would pray...occasionally, I think? Well, she would claim to do so anyway. I wouldn't call her out on it, honestly. But she called me out on it if I didn't. It's not like we had spirituality as a foundation of our relationship, so it was more of a weird way of nitpicking.

Phoenix: Ooooh my goodness, Chris would read the Bible and write notes! This one time, we went to my family's church. This was the second or third time we attended. He was fidgeting, sweating, and could not keep still. I was like, look at this demon. [laughs] He couldn't stand to be there.

Ginger: "Look at this demon"...hahaha...DONE!

DIFFERENT STRAINS OF THE NARC VIRUS

Glynn: All that said, what I am really concerned about are the patterns I am seeing in these people. I mean, they are similar but different. Of all the experiences we have discussed, I feel that there are clear disparities between the types of personalities we have encountered. Is it possible that they are like offshoots or different strains of the same narc virus? Covert Narc-teen!

Phoenix: Chris was attention-seeking, grandstanding, superficially charming, lacked reliability, and manipulated most situations; similar to President Trump who is more of an exhibitionist. But Chris was more of the closet type that would sit back in the cut and observe EVERYBODY. I had taken him to a family celebration for the 4th of July. He said he wanted to go, but when we got there, he sat in a chair away from everyone just watching. When I asked if he wanted to play cards or do something, he was like naw. President Trump would have been the life of the party. But Chris was seeking sympathy by sitting alone and looking sad-faced. My family was enjoying the party and ignoring the party-pooper; which frustrated Chris, causing us to leave the party earlier than I normally would have. But when we got in the car to go home, he had so much to say about EVERYBODY. Like he was above the peasants and he was the king of the court; but he was more like the court jester. [laughing robustly]

107

Ginger: Yep, they study you...your circle...find your triggers, likes, and dislikes. Watching you and the people you hang around gives them more insight so they know how to manipulate you. There's ALWAYS a calculation on their part.

Glynn: There are elements of that in Simone. But there is something malicious about her. This is gonna sound--fuck it, I'll just say it. That bitch scares me!

Phoenix: Really? Scares you how?

Glynn: I ain't scared she'd whoop my ass or anything. She'll try me like she could, though. Ha! It's more of her mindset. She was constantly causing confusion and chaos. To be more precise, it's like I feel threatened. Like everything she does is meticulously done to harm me. Even when she is being playful, it's like she is trying to hurt me.

Ginger: Trust me, that IS the case. Simone is quite toxic! I'm always side-eyeing her and her motives.

Glynn: There were multiple times where she pulled a butcher knife out of the kitchen drawer after joking back and forth, play wrestling, or just as a show of force. And it ain't like I thought that shit was cute. I told her to cut it out numerous times. Sometimes, I would even have to wrestle the knife out of her hand just so I could feel safe. It never made sense. That ain't what scares me about her, though. It's how she mentally and emotionally tries to corner me. Pushing me into a fight, flight, or freeze mode. She loves goading people, as if she wants to provoke you to retaliate. In private, in public, stranger, friend, child, me, you-- it doesn't matter!! And what's more, she will convince you it wasn't her fault. And THAT'S what terrifies me! Her ability to get away with the bullshit. I watched my friends and family turn on me due to some chaos she started; only to have her justify her own actions and have my people back her up. It's insane!! I have only seen a couple of people check her and one was a judge. The other was some random dude at a movie theater who chin checked her vanity. It was hilarious. But other than that, she is aggressively combative. Anyone else that stood up to her, all got shut down. There is a strong malfeasance emanating from her. Like she enjoys turning people against each other.

Ginger: Your family and friends turning on you was part of her plan. Narcissists go on a smear campaign to make others look at you as the villain. They'll tell others what you said about them during pillow talk or make up stories to get others to turn on you. Even if you tell them that she pulled a knife on you, she'll manipulate and gaslight that incident, making you look like a bitch; emasculating you in the process. That smear campaign is real fucked up, but reaps great benefits to their purpose, which is your destruction!

Phoenix: Wait, so Simone pulling a knife out on you was not scary? I don't know? [scratching my head and shrugging my shoulders] I would have been scared or at least felt threatened. I think I would have killed her at that point! But I have a little temper myself. I have pulled a gun on one of my ex-boyfriends. There was an incident with Chris once where he put his index finger to my forehead. I was at his front door ringing the doorbell. He didn't answer, so I was walking from the porch back to my car. As I got to the walkway, he came out of the house and told me to get out of here. I thought to myself, "Really? I'm already leaving so you could have stayed in the house at this point." He then put his index finger to my forehead and said, "Don't come back here ever again." I looked him square in the eyes and told him to never put his fucking hands on me again or I would kill him. I also said, "Ok, you sure this is what you want?" He had this look on his face as if he regretted his action, then said, "That's what I said!" I walked to my car and skirted off. He called me later to apologize. I figured he had a female in the house and was grandstanding.

Glynn: I can believe that. It is more common for a woman to pull a weapon on a man. In most cases, that is seen as a woman defending herself from a greater threat. I am not one to hit a woman, though. Contextually, she was "playing" most of the time she did it. But it put me in an awkward position.

Phoenix: Naw, you don't play with weapons. To me, you must want to die by pulling a weapon out on me. [In Ice Cube's voice] Shit, I'm from Detroit. P.A. baby! Yay yay! [laughs with serious intent]

Glynn: [laughs] That is true. But you have seen the movie *Enough*, right? With Jennifer Lopez? Or a more recent film like *Gone Girl* with Ben Affleck?

Phoenix: I did see *Enough* but I am unsure if I watched *Gone Girl*.

Glynn: Phoenix, when I finished watching *Gone Girl*, I was like, "Ah, shit...That's gonna be me, ain't it?" The whole movie, everything the husband's character did just framed him in a bad light. He was seen as a villain for nearly 2 hours because what else could he be? [sarcastically speaking] It's not like he was a victim. That would be preposterous! That said, it's easy to say that I should've molly-whopped her (Simone) one time. But doing so would leave me in what position, exactly? As a man, I dunno...it's hard to explain.

Ginger: WOW! I have never experienced any form of violence from DeWayne. The most I've experienced was disrespectful name-calling and that happens rarely. I never felt afraid of him, although he's always said how "tough" he is. He is meek, to a degree, which makes him seem less threatening. DeWayne is more covert with his bullshit, flying just under the radar. This is why he gets away with his narcissistic abuse so easily.

Glynn: You say covert, but his behaviour never became exaggerated? So would you liken his narcissism to a crocodile submerged in a river?

Ginger: Hmmm, I guess so. He's very sneaky and does things with a sleight of hand. As I stated earlier--figuratively speaking--he kills you by death with a thousand cuts. He'll insult your whole family by making comparisons of "other" people, but is actually talking about you. He loves left-handed compliments. But in public, around others, he'd glorify the hell outta you. In private, he'll belittle your entire being.

Glynn: I see. Simone would pull that BS. She had a habit of taking advice or information that I gave her just to ignore it or criticize it. Then she would get the same thing said to her by someone else and it is like sage wisdom or some shit. I was like, "Uh, you know

I told you the same thing before, right?" But of course, she wouldn't remember me talking to her at all. She had more memory loss than Guy Pierce's character in *Memento*. Dewayne, on the other hand, seems adept at the art of illusion. He is basically like a street magician.

Ginger: Yes! Old DAVID COPPERFIELD ASS! He had me trapped in his web for a short minute, but his mask started to fall off after a few months. The Covert/Closeted Narcissist can keep themselves hidden in plain sight because they can imitate, mimic, and fake many of our emotions, empathy, and other likable character traits. They put on this facade of caring, generosity, love, devotion, and other feelings that we want our partners to possess. Their fake epiphanies and revelations are cards ready to be played when the need arises. Only when you cross them do you start to see the real them. And after faking it for so long, they start to relax and their true selves start to be revealed. It's a shock to your soul when that MUTHAPHUKKA appears! My heart sank when the real SLIM SHADY stood up!

Phoenix: I agree with you, Ginger. The fact is that covert or closet narcissists are really self-absorbed. Nothing matters if it doesn't involve them. They get bored easily or they feel people or things are unworthy of their attention. They will even ignore you if they feel the conversation is not worth their time. Chris would do this to me frequently. We could be having a conversation then he would start playing a game on his cell phone or begin a new conversation in the middle of my sentence. As if to say, "Fuck what you're talking about."

Ginger: STOP!!! [shakes head in disbelief] I told you that Chris and DeWayne were the same person! [laughs] They operate from the same playbook. Both are closeted narcs! Weirdest shit ever! But, Glynn, you have a straight maniac on your hands. She's the most toxic one of all, it seems.

Phoenix: Simone is the type that will kill you, hide your body under the porch, then call the police to report you missing all with tears in her eyes. She is the toxic strain of the narc virus.

Ginger: The crazy bitch would even join the search party!

Glynn: Funny you mention the police because that is like her trump card. One time she got into it with Kenny and called me over. I was at the hospital with Noah waiting on her to come back. When she called, I was like, "Where are you?" She told me she called the police on Kenny cuz they got into a fight. I was like "What the fuck happened?" She didn't elaborate and just asked me to come over there. When I arrived, two officers were already there. Now I am nervous and stupefied by this. I walked into the house to see them talking to Kenny. After a while, I was like, "I'm gonna go." But she told me to wait. I felt there was not much to add to what the officers were saying. Even when I did, she would just interrupt me and the cops just to say she already told Kenny something we were saying. Me and the cops were kinda like, why are we even here? At that point, I kept trying to leave, but she kept insisting I stay until after the cops left. When they left, me and Kenny were having a discussion but Simone would chastise Kenny which upset him. When he flared up, I stepped in to defend her. Now, me and Kenny were yelling back and forth. The fucked up thing was, Kenny and I weren't angry at each other--hell, I didn't even wanna be there--but she wouldn't let either of us leave until we were in direct conflict with one another. It was fucked up... Afterward, I was confused about the whole ordeal. I wasn't even really clear what they fought about. Just that hands were put on one of them by the other. But she just calmly let me know that I could go back to the hospital to tend to our sick son. Which I did, carrying the weight of all that manufactured aggression and negativity. Energy I didn't even have when I arrived there in the beginning.

Phoenix: I feel like she set you up to take the heat off her. She knew Kenny would be mad at her after the police left. So, in her passive-aggressiveness, you were made the target of his anger. This is a classic move of the toxic strain. It's like playing Three-card Monte where the victim is tricked into betting their emotions or feelings on the assumption they can find a healthy relationship.

Ginger: Absolutely!!

Glynn: THAT'S JUST IT, THOUGH!! It is so obvious looking back at it, but when you're in the moment, it is hard to decipher her motives. And her ability to take your reaction and turn you into a crazy person, making it seem as though you are overreacting-- it is maddening and terrifying. She will push, and push, and push; she wants to drive you to hit her. I am smarter and more resilient than that, though. But she gets so...hostile! It is like I have a rabid dog barking at me on a chain. She will invade my personal space, insult me, and threaten me. Everything. She likes to provoke an attack, though. She won't just hit you unprompted. She is too clever. She needs probable cause to initiate an attack. It doesn't have to be anything major. If I grazed her trying to get past her, then she would shove me. If she gets in my face and I tell her to back up, she would respond with, "Or else what?" This was constant. After a while I felt like a seagull in an oil spill; covered in toxic shit, unable to fly, and cornered; unable to escape.

Phoenix: Most people don't believe men go through this shit. If they tell their true story, they are seen as weak or told to "man up" or "you need to check your bitch." Not knowing the constant blaming and shaming a female puts them through. Sometimes, a woman's tongue can cut like a machete causing self-doubt. Glynn, did you ever begin to believe the things Simone said about you were true?

Glynn: [Exhales deeply] Yes. It is the most evident in the case of Noah. She makes me feel like I am not a good father. She boxes me out, then blames me for not being around. Convincing everyone that was in my inner circle that I am a weak, pathetic, deadbeat. Her words. And after weeks of separation from my son, I started to believe it. Even going as far as to internalize those words.

Ginger: Well, she accomplished what she set out to accomplish. Their entire existence in your life is to destroy what's beautiful in it. Your relationship with your son is the most beautiful thing that you have. He's your reason, your why, your purpose! She knows it and she's doing everything in her power to burn you with it...What a nasty, toxic, psychologically-damaged bitch!

Glynn: [Chuckles] Is that the clinical term for the type of narc I am dealing with?

Phoenix: Well, she is toxic! While dealing with Chris I had to learn what I was up against. Apparently, there are three types of narcissist: the exhibitionist, closet/covert, and the toxic narc. The toxic type is likened to sociopaths and/or psychopaths. There is some overlap in the behaviors as you can tell by our experiences but they each have distinctive traits.

Ginger: I'm convinced that Simone is the toxic type! Hell, I'm SURE I dated a sociopath or two, myself!! BOYYYYY, do WE know how to pick em?!

Glynn: I would be inclined to agree, but it was indeed her who chose me.

Phoenix: I know I have a broken picker. Unfortunately, I picked Chris and a few other guys I dated that have the SAME traits. I think I should just move to a cave because I am magnetically attracted to narcs. Part of me enjoys the challenge and the charm of them, while the other side is screaming, "Run like the hellhound Cerberus is hot on my tail!" But silly me would stop to try and pet his beautiful three-headed ass. Speaking of beauty, Chris was preoccupied with his looks. Chris and I were going to a Will Downing concert at Chene Park. He was wearing a beige short outfit. As we were walking from the car to the venue, he noticed a small stain on his shirt. He had a fit. He said, "I can't go to the concert looking like this. My clothes are dirty. I have to go home." I told him, "No one can see it and it's going to be dark soon. Hell, I didn't see the spot until you mentioned it." He made a big production of it. I was so pissed off and he knew it. So, we drove him back home. He thought I was staying home with him. I said, "Ok, see you later." Him, "Where you going?" Me, "To the concert. Oh, you thought I was staying here with you after I bought these tickets before I met you? Not going to happen." Shiiiiiiiiiddddddddddddddddd, one monkey don't stop the show. I didn't know who was going with me, but somebody was going. I called one of my childhood friends to go to the concert with me. We had a great time! Chris was lounging on the couch without a care in the world when I got back home. He asked, "How was the concert?" I said, "You would know if you had been there." He said, "I saw your pictures and video on Facebook." I did not respond. I went upstairs to get undressed, took a shower, and retired for the night. Apparently, Chris slept on the couch that night because the next morning, I was in bed alone. I slept so well and woke up refreshed. Chris gave me the silent treatment and I was cool with that.

Ginger: Yeah, you had to be punished for leaving him at home. Those are other tools in their arsenal: Silent Treatments and Discards. DeWayne was pretty vain, too. His vanity wasn't his looks, per se. His vanity is his ability to fix everything. He's quite crafty with his hands. He's a regular jack of all trades. This dude could fix just about anything. Every time he fixed a damn near impossible situation, he would gloat, pat himself on the back, talk about how skilled he was, and how no one could do it better. It was amazing to watch him suck his own dick with such tenacity and skill. He'd bust plenty of nuts talking about his greatness. I don't know why I bothered fucking him. My lips couldn't match the magical lockjaw that his DSLs created. I might have been a little jealous.

Phoenix: What the hell is DSL? Dick sucking lips?

Ginger: You damn straight! [laughs]

Glynn: Ummm, I ain't sure how comfortable I am with this topic of excessive self-fellating. [laughs] But I get what you mean. It is overcompensation for sure, but also an announcement of how great they perceive themselves. Like, "If no one else will acknowledge my greatness, I will!" I hate it. Having confidence is not uncommon. I have a fair amount when it's not being drained by Simone. I will say she is vain in a similar way to Chris about her own looks. Pretty sure I have already mentioned that. I am not sure about her "skills" or abilities though. Whenever she wants to pat herself on the back, it's mostly about…well, anything. No matter how minuscule or major. Overall, she just has to be great. The main source of her pride is her physical appearance and her motherhood. She is like…I don't know…a MILF? That is the best way I can think to put it. [laughs in embarrassment]

Phoenix: [rolling eyes inside my head] Oh my goodness, Glynn, I forget how special you are with your virgin ears. [chuckling] Wait! You think she is a MILF? Are you saying her beauty and motherhood attracted you to her?

Glynn: Well that is not what I meant, but yeah. I was trying to explain how her vanity is divided. MILF is just the best term I could think of at the moment. Everything she does is in service of being a pretty mother. I rarely heard people compliment her, but I always heard about who complimented her, from her.

Ginger: [laughing] That's her way of saying you're replaceable. For DeWayne, his greatness needed to be acknowledged. He was grandiose, in a sense...better than everyone else...more intelligent. His way was always the best way. He even knew more than others about situations that he had no experience in. He has his MD, Ph.D., Psy.D, ED, JD, DDS, and ABCD. I'm a teacher of students with special needs. He knew more than me about how to work with my students. I'm also a recovering alcoholic. He was educating me on how I should have handled that situation and had he been with me, I wouldn't have had that issue. Shidddd, I'm surprised his narc ass hasn't started me back to drinking.

Glynn: Everything is driven by their own inflated egos. I honestly stopped trusting anything Simone would say. She often tried to offer me assistance or even suggestions when it came to work and life goals. I was always leery of her insistence to "help me." The caveat to all of her motivations was that it was mostly self-serving. She wanted a butler and a doormat. But she had to lure me in first. Because traditional tricks didn't work. She resorted to turning tricks in the bedroom to keep me entranced and engaged. As long as I was physically attracted to her, she felt she could do or say what she wanted. She would set these awkward boundaries and cross them as a means of trying to show her dominance over me. Sometimes, I would hear her say to her friends that she considered herself different in what kind of guys she likes. Her friends didn't quite understand her taste in men, but I did. There was a conversation when she contested that she isn't into the typical guy, but more into "nerdy" types of men. "Nerdy" isn't the word though. It's more like she liked non-confrontational men. If you couldn't be manipulated in any way, then you were put aside until she found a way. Simone isn't especially misunderstood. She is just a predator.

Ginger: She likes men that she can dominate and then will emasculate you for allowing her to be domineering. If you stand up to her, she pushes the limits farther until you break. Then, once broken, you lose it, showing fragility. At that point, you're nothing but a bitch who can't handle "strong" women...And the cycle continues.

Glynn: Pretty much.

Phoenix: Chris thought he was misunderstood or special in some way. He would often say, "No one understands me. That is why I stay to myself." But in actuality, his problems were no different than anyone else's. He wanted to be special and used it to gain sympathy. He was also veeeeerrrry sensitive to criticism. If he was corrected or told he did something incorrectly, he would oftentimes explore or flee the situation. The other person was always stupid and didn't know what they were talking about. This included his supervisors and co-workers with years of experience. He never could see the role he played in conflict and God forbid he acknowledge he was wrong for anything. During our nine-month relationship, he had three or four different jobs he was fired from. According to him, everyone was lazy because he outworked them all or no one knew what they were doing. He didn't get along with his co-workers because, "None of them are on my level," according to Chris. He would say he was the supervisor's favorite worker because of his hard work ethic. Please, how much of a favorite could he be if he was fired from EVERY job. Aww man, even his mother would tell him he was special and smarter than people thought. Come to think of it, the women in his family treated him as if he were special and the younger males admired or feared him as if he were some kind of God. It was both entertaining and intriguing to watch once I realized I was dealing with a narc. They perpetuated his behavior and his idea of being special and misunderstood. I would hear stories of how he was different as a child and treated differently by their father. It was almost like they were protecting him but fearing him at the same time. They kind of stroked his ego to stay on his good side. As the relationship began to unravel, I was repulsed by his and their behavior.

Ginger: These incidences sound so eerily familiar, especially the criticism part. DeWayne hated being corrected. I'm a grammar Nazi, so I would often correct his grammar (I was also being an asshole, but so what). He would always say, "Oh, I know, I know! I'm just texting, so it doesn't matter." After a while though, he would come to me to look over things before sending them out. He had succumbed to my superior grammar skills [laughs]. Anyway, he would always have to be right about everything. And he, too, was the best worker at the job. I came to realize that childhood trauma is what caused so much of his abnormal mental development. His mother loved the word stupid and would use it on everyone and everything. He told me about bringing home a bad report card and being called everything stupid under the sun. He said that changed him for the better and he never brought home another bad grade. Unfortunately, DeWayne didn't see it changed him for the worse. He wanted to be right in everything. He wanted, NEEDED, everyone to see how smart he was. It was like he was saying, "Look mom, I'm not stupid...look, let me show you...let me show everyone!" It became so obvious that I stopped fighting him about things and would do it HIS way, just because I knew he needed to feel smart. To this day, DeWayne still tries to impress his mother, who still shits on him at every turn. They've stopped talking for now, but DeWayne confided in me that he kept staying around in hopes that his mother would eventually love him like she loves her other children. I guess narcs do have feelings, too.

Glynn: That is uncharacteristically candid of him to say. I never thought that DeWayne would be so vulnerable. Wow...I mean, I am skeptical of it, but I don't know. It's in those moments that it's like your empathy is being turned against you. That is the exact moment when you feel compelled to fill a role that is empty. I mean that is how I felt with Simone. Unlike DeWayne, she had a tendency to overshare certain things. Because of that, I didn't know what was personal or common. Most of the things discussed sounded traumatic. At least that is what stands out in my memory. But she would say things so casually sometimes that I was never for certain if it affected her. Her childhood and relationships were all sketchy sounding at best. I rarely, if at all, saw her vulnerable. It felt a lot like she was running from her feelings. I never got a genuine beat on her feelings. She only expressed annoyance, irritation, frustration, dissatisfaction, and anger most times. When she was happy in some way, it was fleeting. But I swear to you, I treasured those moments; no matter how seemingly insignificant. There was much I wanted to explore with her regarding everything she ever told me. But she never liked to revisit those topics. In fact, she told me things that if I mention in future conversation would infuriate her. And it wasn't a matter of me using information against her to win an argument. She was angry that I knew something about her, or her past, that she told me. It was as if she told me things that she wanted me to know but also forget. And knowing anything about her that she willingly shared was a violation of her privacy- - The fuck? I just don't get that woman. From what I could gather though, her toxicity is rooted in deep, unresolved trauma. Such that it is simultaneously holding her back and pushing her forward.

Phoenix: I disagree, Glynn. I think these individuals share their personal traumatic experiences to gain sympathy. There is also the commonality of some form of childhood abuse or traumatic experience. It appears they are the eternal victim condemned to be the martyr of their self-fulfilling prophecy. Because of their past experiences, they believe the world and people owe them something. But the thing that baffles me is they are super sensitive. This sensitive side made me want to hold Chris and protect him from the world.

Ginger: That's how I felt when DeWayne confessed that he just wanted his mother's love. I believed him. I still do, kinda. I've seen that wench in action and the pain in his face when he had a negative encounter with her. She is pure evil and her tactics are sharper than his because she's had more practice. She's also a female narc; bat fucking shit crazy! Against him, SHE ALWAYS WINS!

AMANDA WALLER

Glynn: Simone is a walking contradiction. Just a Tootsie Pop made of concrete with a trauma-filled center. Every lick makes your tongue bleed. Every bite cracks your teeth. But I wanted to help her heal, even at the cost of my own health. In the end, though, scraping against that concrete wall eventually saw me taking on similar traits as her. It kind of became a matter of survival at some point. Like I had to fight fire with fire.

Phoenix: Yes, I noticed a shift in my interactions with Chris as well! For example, I love a good-spirited debate but I don't like to argue. Chris said he didn't like to argue either but that was not the case. It was like he would do or say things just to get a rise out of me. Over time, I fed into his demands. At first, I would speak in a calm tone and ask questions for clarity. About six weeks into the relationship, I was in a full combat zone.

Ginger: I figured that if you can't beat 'em, join 'em. When I say I gave DeWayne nothing, I mean nothing…I could be wrong as two left shoes, but I'd either deflect, project, or gaslight his ass until what we were originally arguing about was a distant memory. He started tripping on me, trying to get me to see his side. I stayed in my bullshit or I'd drop it and tell him that I was done talking about it. I'd use the "I thought you loved me, but clearly you don't" angle. I knew that would get a rise out of him because he wanted so bad to prove that he did. Then we'd talk about that and life went on. I had already told him that he was a narcissist and pointed out why. Next thing you know, he was calling me one, saying I was doing everything I accused him of. It started becoming comical. I became ONE with Narc-man.

Glynn: [in an Emperor Palpatine voice] Gooood, Ginger. I can feel your hate. Let the Narc flow through you.

Phoenix: For me it was different. I was outgoing and a people person before the relationship. I hung out with family, friends, and attended many social events; a complete extrovert. Being with Chris, I became socially withdrawn. Mainly because he was so jealous. I just didn't want to hear his mouth and accusations of me cheating or looking at another man. I buried myself in my studies and hardly left the house. Chris became the center of my world.

Glynn: Same here. I went from being the friend that people could contact day or night to having people sending me an S.O.S. to see if the coast was clear. I have been cussed out just for using my phone at the "wrong times"--any time basically. After a while, just having the phone on my person was a sin for some reason. And if you had a vagina, you were a bitch. Hell, Simone called my goddaughter a **heifer**! And she was only a year old at the time. It was this constant stress that caused an amount of anxiety to build in me that was unprecedented. I became more reclusive and unreachable. Meanwhile, a bunch of my male friends began fraternizing with Simone. So while I was losing friends, she was gaining them. All the while, I was just trying to acclimate to her environment.

Ginger: Actually, Glynn! It's not hate. It's survival. But, from listening to your story and the encounters with Simone, it's hard to discern which of you is the true narcissist or are both of you on the spectrum. For me, I didn't change much. I'd have anxiety at times, but I refused to let him take me back to that dark place where alcohol took me. I worked hard on my self-esteem after I stopped drinking and I wasn't going to have it lowered by some asshole. I even quit smoking cigarettes while dating him. I fought for my life in AA and a detox center. I wasn't losing myself again. Although DeWayne was addictive, I could take it or leave it. But I preferred to take it in doses.

Glynn: Simone wanted me to compromise so much of who I was that it never occurred to me when these changes took effect. They started off as me just being around more to help her. She is a very proud woman, so she never struck me as a wounded puppy or kitten. Simone is more like a wounded scorpion or rattlesnake. In the moments where she was happy, I thought I was helping her heal. But she would be quick to strike out of nowhere. As if to remind me that she is never too happy to sting or bite. And that venom? Whew, boy is it dangerous! Narc venom is like an anti-neurological agent, rewriting your way of thinking, feeling--hell, even being! I found myself in many precarious situations using *her* logic to justify what I knew was wrong.

Phoenix: Between Chris and working on my degree, I had no self-esteem. I mean, I was holding leadership positions and mentoring others in my field, but I began to question my abilities. Even to the point of considering dropping out of school. My head was so fucked up! I didn't know if I was coming or going. I would find myself crying for no apparent reason. And I mean ugly crying with snot running down my chin. Oftentimes, I wondered what *I* had done to be in this position. Some days, I would look into the mirror and truly did not recognize the person looking back at me. My hair was thinning, my weight had dropped, and my eyes looked dull.

Glynn: Wow. Man, I am telling you that Narc venom works in some weird ways. But it definitely causes some self destructive changes.

Phoenix: Ginger, you said, "I didn't change much," but I noticed a change in you. The one thing I noticed is you don't talk on the phone when DeWayne is around. And Glynn, I agree with Ginger. You have traits that are very similar, if not spot on, with a narcissist. Sometimes the signs are so subtle that we don't notice them. I did this with Chris as well. I limited my conversation with people, shut out others, and tailored my conversations to keep Chris out of my business. Sometimes I felt like I was talking in morse code. I found myself only talking to my mother and godsister. It was like a part of me wanted to melt away to please Chris. Like I was a child saying, "Look what I did for you."

Ginger: I don't want him in my conversation. His nosy ass is looking for shit to use against me. I'm pretty much an open book. But I know that he'll twist my entire conversation. It's only with him that I'm different. I can't stand his ass! Ugh!

Glynn: [laughs] That's the point though! It's like being in jail and he is your C.O. Your phone calls are limited to who is deemed acceptable. Hell, I was only allowed to talk to my mother frequently. And if she called too often to check on me, I was a momma's boy. When I call you Ginger, I am no longer "Glynn." But I become every woman, like some throwback Whitney Houston track. [chuckles]

Phoenix: With all that said, it's still a change that should not be ignored. We justify our behaviors to others to make it make sense in our minds. For example, Glynn you have a tendency to be self-absorbed and you reject criticism.

Ginger: Hmmmm...That's interesting, Phoenix. I've been wondering how Simone was able to manipulate EVERYONE in your life, Glynn. Maybe you should take a step back and reflect. You've stated that you identify a lot with DeWayne. This could be a sign that you suffer from NPD, as well. As it relates to changes, Phoenix, I can agree with you on that, but I was looking at major changes. I feel like I fought off what he planned for me, which was complete devastation and annihilation. Although I was hurt by him, he didn't destroy me, but he did teach me a lot more than what I bargained for. But those minor cuts probably do more damage. I don't know. Maybe I'm in denial, but he ain't winning!

Glynn: Nah, doc! It's major and minor changes; which one doesn't matter. The thing that pissed me off was how I changed my views on cheating. When I caught Simone in all her lies, the old me would have burned that bridge with that bitch standing dead in the center of that mofo. But instead, I cussed and swore at her all night. Then I set a thirst-trap for Tre to meet up and almost got into a physical fight with that jackhole. He even told me I was mad at the wrong one. Which was true *and* false at the same time. Hmph, weird. But even with all that, I took her back. What is worse, I started to let her back in my heart. Albeit slowly and over time. Still, it was something that was far removed from the person I was.

Phoenix: Umm-hmm, I fell into this category too! I accepted the cheating from Chris. The first time I caught him texting another woman was the sign. I confronted him, but that was all. This opened the door for him to continue his actions. Then it moved to late-night conversations, hell, even during the day. After that, it was "working" at a nightclub. But he never was paid for his "work." I knew he was meeting women at the club, but I ignored it. Normally, I would have left his ass after I cussed him out. Something about Chris had me under a love spell. Nothing he did could cause me to leave him. I wanted to be with him and all his faults. I became submissive to his will.

Glynn: Oh, I feel you. I wanted to leave but I wanted to stay, too. So, instead of leaving fully, I just engaged in the same surreptitious behavior that she inflicted on me. I became increasingly aloof and reserved. I was confrontational and defensive. I would meet women and go on secret out of town trips. The difference is...that shit was exhausting for me. I guess it's easier when you can manipulate people to cover your tracks and lie to your face. But when it is just you doing it, it's like trying to run a corporation single-handedly. Overall, it was just me trying to leave the abuse without actually getting out of the relationship.

Ginger: Well, I've dated all the narcs! I keep my guard up and it takes the moving of heaven and earth to get past my walls. I think this helped me to cope. Please understand, I know that I was/am narcissistically abused and I suffered plenty, but I'm not claiming victimhood. I'm claiming victory.

Phoenix: It's not that you are a victim but you have accepted DeWayne's behavior. If I'm not mistaken, DeWayne cheated on you with Amber. Is this a behavior you found acceptable or just acceptable with DeWayne? The truth is the three of us have changed from being in relationships with these vampires. They suck our souls with each moment we allow them to stay in our life. We rationalize and justify our changed behavior to minimize our reality. I'm not trying to call you out because we all have done it. But we have to be real with ourselves. It is never easy looking within and defining the role we played in their continued treatment and behavior we allowed.

Glynn: You make a great point. Every time we look for a reason to keep investing in them, it is a compromise with who we are. Even a slight change in an unhealthy direction is enough to qualify as a Narcissistic Infection. What we have endured is not trivial, but most people think it is. I got another example I want to share real quick. The other time was when Simone had ME arrested. All because I took my son to see my mom. I had him while she was outta town. She called to see where I was. I told her I had to run out and took Noah to see my mom. She flipped out and cussed me out. Then she called my mom and cussed her out. When she came back later that evening, I was trying to leave but she stood there defiant, blocking the door; all the while berating me, and trying to provoke me. I largely ignored her, trying not to exchange petty insults...[sighs]...I asked her to move, she didn't. So I escorted her out of the way. She called the cops and had me arrested. Now, I NEVER attacked her or even mishandled her. The police confirmed that she was unharmed. But purely because I touched her first, they arrested me. It was horrifically frustrating. I sat powerless as I was handcuffed for trying to escape a place of vile toxicity. And when I got out, she had the nerve to say, "You only out because of what *I* told them."

I was like, "Bitch!! I was only there because of what you told them!!" She was so smug about it. It was revolting and infuriating. But the most vexing thing, as a man, is how no one believed me. She paints the picture of me being some melodramatic victimized antagonist. When all I ever did was send out cries for help. Instead, people blamed me for sticking around and sided with her for the mistreatment of me. After some time, people stop caring about the "supposed abuse". And eventually, so did I. I stopped caring about me and became obsessed with trying to redeem myself in her eyes. It just led to more mental and emotional abuse. After a while, Simone didn't even need to be present. If we didn't speak, the anxiety of what she would say was enough to perpetuate the stress and depression. But no one understood. To anyone else, I guess it just looked like a boy too weak to be a man. Ugh, fuck people's perception. I was operating at 2% of mirth at all times. It was a change that I had become ok with. And I was NOT ok with that.

Phoenix: I must admit that I even started to think you were the narcissist in the relationship. That you were causing issues then

132

running to say, "Look what she did to me." Hearing your stories were exhausting, which made me not want to talk to you. Sometimes, I even thought you were not telling what you did to cause such actions from Simone. Especially when advice was offered to you but you did not use it.

Glynn: I know. And the funny thing is, I tried!! It's like she hacked my brain and stole my heart. And I don't mean in the romantic sense. I mean, it was like she was an expert thief that cracked the safe my heart was in and took it when I wasn't looking.

Phoenix: Like Amanda Waller from Suicide Squad. How she held the Enchantress's heart in that briefcase to control her.

Glynn: [laughs] It was kind of like that, too. She even stabbed me in the heart--emotionally anyway--when I didn't act like the Narc she wanted me to be. Saying virtually anything to hurt me. So, in turn, I just internalized it. I was either skulking around and being a gigolo. Or I was in a dark place, pining for "My precious" like Smeagol from Lord of the Rings. Either way, I wasn't doing what I *knew* was healthy for me. And all I did was end up becoming unfamiliar with myself.

Phoenix: At times I questioned if it was me? Am I narcissistic? I didn't feel like myself. I was overly sensitive to criticism. I felt nothing I did was right. I was apathetic toward others. Then I realized I was becoming who Chris wanted me to be; a reflection of him.

Ginger: I never felt that I was losing myself. I always fought off his attempts to belittle me and lower my self-esteem. I know I was victimized, but I just never felt less than because of what he did to me. I bucked against him at every turn. DeWayne could kiss all of my round ass.

Glynn: That question often plagued me, though. It still does really. There are still times I am unsure whether or not I am. Like, how do you know it isn't you? Is it a reflection? Shit, I don't know--It's more like being in a house of mirrors sometimes.

Ginger: Yeah, you were in the funhouse! [laughs]

Phoenix: Right! You walk around trying to figure out which is your true reflection. I felt like I was trapped in my body, struggling to get out. I was walking but the steps were not my own. My thought process was restructured piece by piece to think like Chris. Instead of "What Would Jesus Do?" it was "What Would Chris Do?" It was a maze of confusion that I was not familiar with. I would even ask him what he thought before I made a move. I would take him shopping with me to get his approval of my clothes. I was really gone! I guess my rationale for wanting his approval on my attire was because when we went out with his friends, they were complimenting me which made Chris jealous. So, to prevent that, I wanted him to pick my clothes. That way, if his friends said anything, it was on him.

Ginger: [cuing the Twilight Zone music]

Glynn: That is definitely true. Approval from Simone was important. [laughs] Though, I wasn't concerned with what she thought of my clothes. Sometimes we would have discussions and I would find myself siding with her. Not because we were in agreement, but because I thought it was easier to do so. I wasn't sure if she knew I was doing this or not but when I would agree she'd change her opinion almost immediately...Hmmm, come to think of it...There were times when she would pick out clothes for me if we went shopping. When I wore an outfit she suggested and received a compliment, she would take credit for it. I guess I was concerned with what she thought about how I dressed after all. [sighs exasperatedly] Well, that sucks.

Phoenix: Hahaha, the change is so subtle you barely notice it. Even when Chris moved out of my house, he left some of his belongings in order to keep one foot in the door. Normally, I would have told him to get ALL his shit. But I wanted him to keep some things there so he could come back. I guess I needed an excuse for him to come back whenever he wanted. [deep sigh] Talking about it now sounds so sad, depressing, and pitiful. I am ashamed of myself. Why couldn't I let him go? I couldn't choose me over him? I should have hit myself in the head and said, "Bitch, wake up!"

Ginger: WOW! As bullheaded as I know you to be, I'm shocked, somewhat. But I understand, too. That manipulation is real. For me, my mother would always call me *Mary, Mary Quite Contrary*. If you told me to go left, I'm going right. I would never conform voluntarily. DeWayne tried every which way to "get me in line." After a while, he grew so frustrated that he gave up trying. He told me that I was the most stubborn person he had ever met. I never vied for his approval. Maybe because I had lost so much respect for him. I might have even looked down on him, felt pity and disgust at the same time. But, from what I understand, many victims seek to overplease them and feign for their approval.

Maybe, in some way, I did and just don't realize it. But right now, FUCK DeWayne!

Phoenix: Wait, Ginger, do you not recall us having a conversation about whether you were the narc?

Ginger: I remember! [side-eye]

Glynn: Oh, SNAP!!

Ginger: I'm not a narc. I've just adopted some of their bullshit through the experiences I've suffered through. The abused becomes the abuser. I'm the narc slayer! [laughs] But you're funny. [still laughing]

Glynn: [laughs] Alright Buffy. You say that now. But when "Angel" gets done fixing your bathroom, I hope you're ready to stake his ass and close the Hellmouth so he can't come back!

Ginger: [slaps knee] I GOT THIS! Let us pray or prey, depending on who you are!

Phoenix: Trying to make me think I'm the only fucked-up bitch here! Girl, if you don't get off that Nile! Hell, DeWayne is fixing your bathroom right now. What's up with that! And those tools in your basement? He is never leaving.

Glynn: Yeah! He's gonna be there forever. Forever, ever?

Phoenix: Forever, ever...sorry, Ms. Jackson!

Ginger: [laughing hysterically] Mannnn, y'all ain't NEVER lied! Once he cracked the tub, I knew I was back in a long-term relationship! [laughing my fucking ass out] And the tools are the same as with Chris. He needed to have a reason to come back and

I needed my bathroom fixed. So, here I am...in the funhouse, waiting for DeWayne to turn THE FUCK UP!

Glynn: At least you're getting something out of it. I guess, in regards to Chris and Simone, it comes off more like a parasitic situation more so than a symbiotic one.

Ginger: Don't get me wrong, I've definitely given more than I've received! The takers will run all of your pockets if you let them. His fixing my bathroom is payback! But in the meantime, he's using up every damn thing in this house! [sighs]

Phoenix: At least you are getting something. All I got was debt and the feeling as if I wasn't enough. I think I even told him I would follow him anywhere.

Ginger: [laughs] I thought you were going to say debt and dick!

Phoenix: [laughing] That too! He had me singing Drake "The Best I Ever Had."

Glynn: I mean, I got pussy from a dick. I don't even know how that's possible.

Phoenix: I don't know what to say about that. At least you got fucked? But that may have been a bad thing.

Glynn: Yeah, it was. [laughs] I think I would have preferred getting my bathroom redone.

Ginger: Too funny!

Glynn: I gotta say, I had a similar feeling of inadequacy. It wasn't enough to be "even" with her; I felt I owed her because of the way we kept taking breaks from each other. We did whoever we wanted and lied about it to each other. Then we would try to catch the other in a lie. Ugh! It was like Spy vs Spy. That reminds me--Ginger, I wanted to ask something. Didn't you say something about meeting someone when you and DeWayne were on the outs?

Phoenix: Yes, "Buffy," and you took DeWayne back after cheating on you with Amber. That is definitely out of character for you.

Ginger: Yes, I did and yes it was, but I was under the influence!

Glynn: Under the influence of that, DICK! [laughs] Nah, but seriously, though; what was the motivation for returning?

Ginger: You're terrible. [laughs] Well, the man I "met" was someone I knew for a while (before DeWayne). After about 10 months of being free, I fucked him. He visited me from Wisconsin during Spring Break. It wasn't anything serious. In fact, he was a bad fuck and a waste of time. DeWayne love-bombed me about a month or so later. So, it wasn't a motivation to return, but more of a manipulation!

Phoenix: Bullshit! You wanted to pay him back for hurting you.

Ginger: A little! [shrugs]

Phoenix: Hahaha, at least you own it!

Glynn: Yeah, like a tit-for-tat situation. I wish I had all of that as an excuse. I wasn't nearly in the position to hesitate for that long. For me, it was a devour or be devoured scenario. After I found out about Simone's cheating, I felt pressured to get even and get away. I didn't wait for any amount of time. It was as soon as I got the chance. Simone NEVER gave our relationship room to breathe during any hiatus, so neither did I. I had a week at most to find someone new, or old, to fuck around with. She was surrounded by dicks and had the option to choose whoever she wanted. I felt like if I sat around and wasn't proactive, then I would lose the mock war we were having. I acted out in frustration. I wasn't trying to heal. I was trying to hurt. But at the same time, I didn't want her to know. So, I hid what I was doing. Only once were we in a place where I thought we could reconcile was I truthful with her. We weren't doing anything that benefited us. I knew that. I hated myself every time I ever decided to express my "freedom." Simone would claim she had no obligation to me, thus, she was free to do what she wanted. Everyone told me I was free to do the same. But I never felt that way. I was loyal to my feelings by default. So even if we were going back and forth, or whatever, it was in my nature to process those emotions properly. By not doing that and trying to do what she did, it backfired. I felt the weight of everything I was doing reverberate emotionally. My empathy kicked in heavily and I became overcome with guilt, shame, and remorse. Something that I carry with me to this day. I tried working it out with her in part because I felt *I* mistreated her. Even though some would say we were technically even. I don't see it that way. I was wrong and deserved the neglect to some extent.

Phoenix: Yeah, I started messing around too. I was going on dates and spending nights out. I no longer cared what Chris was doing, who he was seeing, or who he did it with.

Ginger: I swear to GAWD I was looking. Nobody wanted me. I think he had some radar on my ass or something, cuz I couldn't find ANYONE to cheat with! But LORD, I WAS looking! Still looking!

Glynn: That's crazy though! Wanting to cheat and cheating is *NOT* what *I* got in a relationship to do. Like, don't get me wrong, part of me feels justified based on the abuse I was subjected to. That doesn't make it right though. It was indeed an act of desperation. Honestly, I found like three women that were viable fresh starts. But I was too invested in the life I had with Simone. Every attempt at escape felt like trying to uproot a tree by myself.

I AIN'T TRYNA' FIX NOBODY

Phoenix: The hardest thing to figure out is if you want to stay in the relationship or how to exit the relationship. For me, I had to exit the relationship for my own sanity. How are you guys feeling about staying or leaving?

Ginger: I think any relationship with a narcissist is toxic and you should get out of it sooner rather than later. It takes an emotionally and mentally strong ass individual to take them on. They are wicked by nurture. I left the relationship for a year, but went back because I obviously love a challenge. My head is hard as hell. With everything I've experienced with DeWayne, I still don't hate him. There were times when I felt I did, but ultimately, I don't. I actually have love for him and I always wish him the best. I've also envisioned him being water-boarded by Russians and fucked with a cactus. But HATE?? Nahhhh, I don't hate him! He's still here, in the love-bomb stage, fixing my bathroom and trying to help cook dinner and clean the house...Just moving in, cuz they ALWAYS have an angle.

Glynn: Wait, "nurture"? Don't you mean "nature"?

Ginger: NOPE! These mofos were created...nothing natural about them!

Phoenix: I'm still on being fucked with a cactus.

Ginger: [laughing my ass off] LITERALLY!!!

Glynn: Hmmm, that is probably why we try to fix them in the beginning. We see the parts of them that were fucked up by others and think it is an easy fix. Just by showing them that there is an alternative to what they have experienced, in us. But instead of pulling them into a rational world, you get hoovered into their illogical one.

Ginger: That's exactly it! We're just a bunch of E-40s, trying to be Captain Save-a-hoe!

Phoenix: I ain't tryna' fix nobody! Shit, I need to be saved and find my Captain-save-a-lady because I ain't no hoe. [laughing]

Ginger: That just went over your head, huh! [slapping forehead]

Phoenix: I'm tired of being the one that has to be the strong one in the relationship. I want someone that can make a decision without constantly asking me for help or being their support system. I need somebody to be there for me; or at least share in our roles.

Ginger: Me too!

Glynn: Well if that is how y'all feel, I am the opposite. I need someone that values my input in the relationship and isn't quick to dismiss me as a curse, instead of a blessing. We all have our strengths and weaknesses, but I feel like what I have experienced is a lack of balance. After numerous attempts at trying to be balanced in a relationship with Simone--and failing--I figured it was time to let it die. I didn't have to do much to solidify that either. I just needed not to attempt reconciliation. Her perception of me did the rest. I am not like Ginger in regards to how I feel about her though. My animosity is dependent on how she is gonna attempt to fuck up my life next. With everything she put me through, she and I can't have a positive outcome without a healthier resolution. Also, I have a son with her. I am pretty sure that means I am stuck dealing with her for life. Ugh! [rolls eyes]

Phoenix: I think I can speak for both Ginger and me, when I say we want balance as well. Part of our narc abuse was inflating our ego only to deflate it in the end. As women, we are looking for something different than you in a relationship. We look for a man that is a provider and a protector. As well as having confidence but is caring at the same time.

Ginger: Precisely! Someone to lead and not into a ditch! I don't want a man-child who can't handle things or one who overhandles things. I need a balance! A happy medium...a non-narcissist! Hell, I've been dealing with these sick bastards so long, I'd fuck up a normally functioning relationship!

Glynn: I can dig that. I couldn't tell you what I am looking for at this point. All I know is that I don't want another Simone. What scares me is that I might have exhausted my capacity to love another woman romantically. Which is just as well, because I also feel like I won't find a healthy and compatible woman to attempt a relationship. Phoenix, you had divine intervention in the Feds taking Chris off of your hands. So, you have freedom to move forward without his interference. That said, what would you have done to exit the relationship if that wasn't the case?

Phoenix: Ummm...the Feds stepping in was the nail in the coffin. I had made a plan to exit the relationship with Chris. Remember, this was only a nine-month relationship. After the first 90-days, I was planning my exit. The first thing I did was gather my support system. I told them what was going on in the relationship to give them a heads-up. At first, they thought I was exaggerating, but then they saw and heard things directly from Chris. Once I had their support, it was time for the next step. What I did next was not taking things personally. This took power away from Chris as I no longer cared about his feelings. Hence, advocating for myself. I made myself the priority in the relationship. I did things I liked and started going out with my friends. I started exercising and other things that gave ME pleasure. I set boundaries for what I was going to do for him and what I was not going to do. I told him he had to call me before coming to my house. I did not do any favors for him. This created a healthy distance between Chris and I as he wanted to be the center of my world. When I started treating him like he treated me, he was confused. I showed no empathy for his issues. When he wanted to argue, I gave him the silent treatment. Then, I did some research and read a few articles on narcissism. I think doing the research was my greatest asset to ending the relationship. The final and most refreshing step was throwing away ALL OF HIS SHIT. I felt like Bernie from Waiting to Exhale; "Get yo' shit, get yo' shit." It is no joke. I really was able to breathe again. My shoulders felt lighter and my soul was at ease. I felt like a new woman. I noticed my confidence had come back and I was gaining weight.

Ginger: Ok. So the Feds sealed it, stopped the hoover and potential love-bombing...Or has he made contact from the cell?

Phoenix: In true narc fashion, yes he did. This ninja called me collect from LaSalle County Jail. It was about two or three weeks after my mother's trip. You know, the one she insisted that Chris go on. He was like, "P, how you doing? I know you mad at me." I said, "No, but my mother is. She wants her money from you that she spent on the trip." Chris said, "Oh, tell mommy I will give her her money back, but I was arrested on my way back home. We was pulled over by the Feds. I didn't know Ross had drugs and money in the truck. I had nothing to do with it. They tryna' charge me but I think I will be out in a few weeks. Do you love me?" "Well, I wish you luck and hope everything turns out well for you. I have to go; this call is expensive." [Click] He called me one more time after that to ask me to check on his mother. I asked him "Why would I do that?" He got mad. I haven't heard from him again.

Ginger: YOU WILL!

Phoenix: I put a block on my phone and he is serving a mandatory 15-years.

Ginger: [laughs] CUTE! You remember my sociopath that I dated in college. He was sentenced to 25 to Life. Somehow he got out in eight. Who did he reach out to? His FAVORITE empath! [laughs ecstatically]

Phoenix: OH SHIT. I almost forgot about him. He even tried to friend me on Facebook. Girl!

Ginger: EXACTLY!!! He used you for a flying monkey, too! So keep your guard up!

Phoenix: Thanks for the warning. But you know I was not going to be no flying monkey for THAT ninja. I couldn't stand him when we were in college. With his lyin' ass.

Ginger: I know! But he TRIED IT!

Phoenix: Yes he did. I feel you. I will keep this in mind. Wakanda forever! [softly hits chest with my arms crossed]

Ginger: [crosses arms and bangs chest] HUUH!

Glynn: Y'all crazy. [laughs]

Phoenix: So Glynn, since you have a child with Simone, it will be hard for you to completely escape her. How do you plan to manage keeping some kind of sanity? I know that you have started going out to events. Is this part of your plan?

Glynn: Ok. Ummm, I don't know. I would say that on my end, I got tired of trying to rally my friends together in preparation for my separation from her. Those people I was claiming as my friends made decisions that were antithetical to our friendship. So I let it go. Simone kind of won in that way. But those relationships were weak, so I suppose it was for the best. Narcs have a way of spreading their infection through people and, in order to stop it, you need to inoculate those closest to you, so that there is a stronger communal immunity. But, those people were anti-vaxxers and I wasn't informed enough to educate them on the toxicity of narcissism. I, like them, just thought it was a matter of regular relationship shit. I had ups and downs, arguments and issues before. You just chalk it up to two people trying to figure each other out. This was reinforced by the same mutual acquaintances of me and Simone. I didn't have a plan and I didn't have a support system in place to help me. That changed once I started working for American Mental Health Services. I learned more about mental health and became better aware of my situation. I started to understand, through conversations with you and everyone else there, that I needed to free myself by not romanticizing the relationship. It was a process that took years, unfortunately. But with the birth of Noah, I finally saw who I was dealing with. By that time though, I had gained a better support system and started taking the advice I was given. Better late than never I suppose. Now I am at the point that I can separate how I feel from what I need to do. I won't allow myself to be hoovered anymore. Although I haven't escaped fully, I have managed to keep my distance and keep the abundant soul sucking confrontations of yesteryear. Now, instead of staying locked away, I have begun going back out and trying to enjoy life. So far I have taken trips, gone to a handful of events, and even started writing again. Anything I can to push forward and be productive.

Ginger: A little advice, Glynn...Research Gray Rock method for when you have no choice but to deal with them (narcs) and follow it to a TEE!

Phoenix: I had to use this method with Chris. I was emotionally non-responsive to his bull crap. I observed instead of engaging. If he asked me questions, I would ask him what does he thinks and I used a lot of "mm-humm" and "uh-huhs." I faded out of the relationship. I also became boring to him. I remember us driving on the Lodge coming from downtown. Chris said, "We don't have fun anymore. I want that back." I said, "If you want us to have fun, then you need to plan something because I'm done." His smile disappeared, he frowned his face, and turned his head away from me. I was offering him NOTHING. I even stopped telling Chris things that were going on in my life. Another thing that helped with distancing from him was me not looking so good. For Chris, I was a show piece. I started dressing in sweats or jeans and t-shirts. This was hard for me because I love to dress nicely and look my best. But, it was necessary. Everyday I looked in the mirror and did positive self-talk. Sometimes, I stood in the mirror totally naked and said out loud what I like or loved about every part of my body; even my fat belly and my childhood scars.

Ginger: Y'all were "on the Lodge wit' it" [laughing out loud].

Phoenix: [laughing hysterically] Girl, you're bananas!

Ginger: No, seriously, that was brilliant on your part. The narc hates no contact or gray rock, unless they're the givers of it, as with the silent treatment. Whenever I would distance myself, DeWayne would get more clingy. I started using that to my advantage to get what I wanted. I noticed he feared being alone. It's funny how extremely fragile they are. It would be times like these that my empathy would go into overdrive. But, I'm also a Cancer, a crab. When you fuck with me, I snap HARD. After a while, I had zero phukks to give and didn't care how he felt or where he was.

Phoenix: So, do you plan on keeping DeWayne around or will you eventually get rid of him forever?

Ginger: [sigh] I don't really know. I know that I will eventually want to get married, but not to him. So, I guess I'll get rid of him at some point. He's a huge fixture in my life. Right now, he's not bothering me too much, but I know that won't last.

Phoenix: He's not bothering you, until he does.

Ginger: Exactly! He loves drama, so I know it's coming. I'll be on the receiving end of his narcissistic abuse within a month.

Phoenix: But you love drama too! So, he gives you your supply as well. When and if you do let the relationship go, how will you do it; especially with keeping a relationship with "what's that boy's name?" With his fine self. [laughing] Is he 18 yet? My inner cougar is coming out.

Ginger: William? And keep your paws away! [laughing out loud] For the LAST TIME, I DO NOT LOVE DRAMA. I'm dramatic!

Phoenix: [laughing loudly] What's the difference?

Ginger: One is messy and natural. The other is acting.

Phoenix: Ok, Drama Queen. Or, should I say best actress in the category of drama? Anyway, what is your plan?

Ginger: I'm going to continue on for now, but will leave eventually. It's hard to say exactly how I'm going to do it. I've left before, but ended up back in it. The first thing I will do is get my finances in order. That's actually my main reason for staying. Financial insecurity is a bitch.

Phoenix: Are you saying you need DeWayne to help pay your bills?

Ginger: No, Phoenix, I'm not saying that. I'm saying that I'm afraid to take everything on by myself. I'm not financially prepared for if something goes wrong. DeWayne will make a way out of no way to ensure that he gets credit for saving me...I mean, to ensure that I'm okay.

Glynn: First of all, both y'alls is crazy. But secondly, Ginger, you have had previous relationships where you took the initiative to leave. How did you get out of those unscathed?

Ginger: UNSCATHED? Oh, you got jokes!

Phoenix: Right, cause you are bat shit crazy! But so am I. [sigh] Naw, but fo' real. No one ever comes out unscathed after being in a toxic relationship.

Ginger: BATSHIT!!

Glynn: Man, whatever! My point IS, she got out before and she can get out again. Hell, she might even be in the sequel.

Ginger: My college psychopath went to jail, like Chris. The other ones either faded out or I pushed away. I've never had a healthy relationship...EVER!

Phoenix: So, do you think you can use any of the gray rock techniques on DeWayne?

Ginger: NO! DeWayne is either all or nothing.

Phoenix: Do you think DeWayne has to end the relationship in order for you to escape? Like Simone did with Glynn.

Glynn: Hold on cuz! You ain't bout to just put me on blast like I just got dropped off at the boyfriend orphanage. That chickenhead didn't "end it"...She just thinks she did!

Phoenix: Ooooookay! [winking my left eye and doing the ok hand sign]

Ginger: [laughing] RIGHT! But, yes, Phoenix! It'll have to be something big, like publishing our entire relationship in a tell-all book!

Phoenix: Really, really Ginger! That's your plan?

Ginger: [wink wink] YOU DAMN SKIPPY!

Glynn: Shit! That wouldn't work. Hell, he would probably take the credit for being the inspiration and use it as a means to stay to work on the relationship like he did your bathroom. Which by the way, won't be done until 2022!

Ginger: Yep! He's the reason for the best-seller and where are his royalties! [laughing] Oh, the bathroom is going great. We're only on month 6 of the 5x5 bathroom--NOT EXAGGERATING! Which reminds me, though, of how I tried to use gray rock towards him, that didn't work. When we split while he was working on my bathroom, he left it gutted. He offered to fix it, but it included being with him, although it was indirectly stated. He came over to work on it and was NASTY acting. I was afraid that he would deliberately sabotage the project. He talked and talked and talked about our relationship so much. I tried my best to ignore it. He figuratively beat me into submission. All I wanted to do was stay focused on the bathroom, which is how gray rock works. You stay focused on the matter at hand and you do NOT discuss anything about your relationship. You only deal with that person briefly and limit side-bar conversations. In your case, Glynn, your interactions with Simone should only focus on Noah. There should be no conversation about how horrible of a father you are or how much of a toxic narcissist she is. It doesn't involve conversations about mutual friends, family, work, school, NOTHING, except Noah and his well-being. When she cuts into you about your "absence," you do not respond or give an explanation. You repeat your question or statement about Noah. "So, does Noah need anything? How was his doctor's appointment? Could you let me know the next appointment date? I'd like to attend." You have to be as plain, bland, and as uninteresting as a gray rock!

Phoenix: That's some good advice. But I think Simone will find a way to engage Glynn since he is a self-proclaimed antagonist.

Glynn: Wait, what?

Ginger: Glynn, you have to figure out how you want this relationship to progress as it relates to Noah and adjust yourself, accordingly. Simone holds great power over you, mentally, to the point that you will cut off your nose to spite your face. As tempting as it is to slay her, you're not the person to do it. You are a great supply for her. She loves to "take you down" and watch you grovel. Every time you open your mouth, her crazy ass is ready to tangle. You have to find a way to ignore her ignorant ass!

Glynn: Well, I am at a loss. But I suppose there is some merit in what is being said. I can't say I see how she can be slayed fully. She ain't a dragon. She is more of a dracula.

Ginger: Well, get your garlic and stake ready!

Glynn: [laughs] Naw, I need holy water and crosses! I should have mentioned this before, but she holds on to shit. So if she is mad at me about anything, she will hold it like a bowel movement during a job interview. Then the next time she sees me face to face, it's going to be word vomit. It's whatever though. I will just try not to get baited into those scenarios.

Phoenix: One thing you must understand is that you can't change her or save her. Her only motivations are her own needs and problems. This will only frustrate you and cause you to be exhausted. Setting and maintaining boundaries can help you keep her at bay.

Glynn: So by "keeping her at bay," should I refrain from talking to my son's siblings, too?

Ginger: Only if you cannot avoid talking to her. She could use them to get to you. She's kind of predatory.

Phoenix: I think holding on to the relationship with Noah's siblings is part of the triangulation. You will need to figure out how to best include or exclude them.

Glynn: Hmmm, ok. I can do that.

Phoenix: Keeping a relationship with them also keeps you pulled into any crisis. Something you need to avoid; except when it involves Noah. He should be your only priority when communicating with Simone. And most of the time, they're crises of her own doing, so why engage?

Glynn: I try to keep the conversations to just Noah, but even then she will limit what information I am given. That is when I get upset. The gray rock approach is an interesting idea, but she actually tries to use that shit on me. And when she isn't, she is withholding what I am "allowed" to know about Noah.

Ginger: You need to try it and STICK to it. The narc is going to always try to take you off your square. That's their mission...to seek and destroy. Gray Rock is hard as hell because they push every button they can and use every tool in their arsenal to get a response. They deflect, project, gaslight, encite, attack, push back, retreat and act sweet in order to get that supply from you. You have to stay strong. She'll try anything.

Phoenix: All that shit is intentional. That is why it will be important for you to choose your battles carefully. She will instigate and goad you into arguments. But, you don't have to engage. Choose to use your time and energy on building a healthy relationship with Noah.

Ginger: Exactly, P!

Glynn: And that is what I want to do. My plan is to get him away from her so that I can build a better father/son bond, sans the watchful eye of Warden Simone. But until I can legally do that, I have to endure this bit of nonsense and tomfoolery a bit longer. [sighs heavily]

Phoenix: I know it may be hard because she appears to have all the control in this situation. She will even try to use your difficulties and what she perceives as your weaknesses against you. So own your issues! She can't use them against you if you claim them first. It's like dealing with a bully or running for a political office. YOU be the narrator of your story.

Ginger: Oh, that's good, Phoenix. That's a great idea. That reminds me of this meme going around that says something like "You can't even insult women anymore. If you call her a bitch, she'll say 'You damn right'...and that's MS. BITCH!" Just own your shit!

Glynn: Soooooooooooo, you want me to pull an 8 Mile on her and just start a rap battle; dissing myself until she gives up?

Phoenix: Exactly! But beware that she may resist. She may bring up old stuff, like you stated, or start a whole new battle. Keeping in true Simone fashion, she will surely throw tantrum a if you choose to ignore her.

Ginger: Now, Mr. Antagonist, be careful not to be assholish about it. She WILL use Noah against you when she's angry. Just go around her bullshit.

Glynn: Bearing that in mind then, I think it prudent to stick and move when it comes to those altercations.

Phoenix: You better "Float like a butterfly and sting like a bee. Her hands can't hit what her eyes can't see."

Glynn: [laughs] Or I could be like water, my friend. Either way, it is about adapting to her heinous attitude. As it stands, I don't have the energy to engage; nor do I have the desire for any discord. I will avoid provocation as best I can. Even if my sheer presence drives her into a tizzy. Her tantrums are so loud and abrasive sometimes that I just want to put her to sleep just so it's quiet.

Phoenix: Don't think of it as adapting to her. You are choosing to make changes for your benefit not her's. This is your plan! Even if you try to not engage or avoid discord, she will try to engage you. It is her nature. She knows no other way. Remember, Simone will NOT change.

Glynn: I know. That is the main thing I keep in mind. Actually, she kind of just tries to tell me that I am more unlikely to change. She has been adamant in calling out that I need to have people to like me, or that I need attention, or I need to feel important. But I am not anything like that.

Ginger: That's typical projection. All of these negative qualities that she says you have are what she hates in herself. She is very bitter from the psychological pain of her past, the pain that she perpetuates in her present, and the pain that she foresees in her future. Remember, hurt people hurt people! I feel sorry for all of them because I know that it's from severe neglect from horrible parents or caregivers, who are only continuing the cycle of this personality disorder. But, we cannot continue to be subjected to their abuse. We have to get out from underneath their pain. We must have a plan.

Phoenix: With that being said, what is your plan?

Glynn: Good question, Phoenix. Do you have a plan for yourself, Ginger? [laughs nervously]

[crickets; long silence]

Phoenix: Do you need us to help you come up with a plan? I know it may be difficult to break from DeWayne since you have a motherly bond with William. If you had never met DeWayne, how would your life be different?

Ginger: I wouldn't have a bonus son. I wouldn't understand that I've been victimized in every relationship. I might not be in Atlanta. I could be married or allowing myself to be loved appropriately. I don't really have a plan. I just want to feel safe and secure. I know that DeWayne is not my soulmate, but there are very strong soul ties.

Glynn: I get that. That is why we are trying to figure out how to help you sever them. If you truly want safety and security, then you will need to first get out of the situation, right?

Ginger: Of course. I guess the urgency isn't there for me, to be honest. I've already discussed my financial insecurities and my need to be more fiscally responsible. That's my biggest hurdle. There's not much more for me to say about that.

Phoenix: There doesn't have to be an urgency. Maybe getting a part-time job to offset your finances could be a plan. The thing is you don't have to act on the plan right now. But, you can start developing a plan. As it stands now, DeWayne is receiving all of the rewards from this situation. What are you really getting out of it, besides a few household chores? Is the stress really worth the end result?

Ginger: I don't know what else you want me to say. But, I've taken the test for Assistant Principal. I'm just waiting to be picked up. Hopefully, I get called soon. That's a nice raise. I'll be taking the test for principal in the next 6 months.

Glynn: Well, how long do you plan to endure his presence? Once William leaves for college, will DeWayne disappear? Will you make an honest effort to cut ties with him and reacclimate to being by yourself?

Ginger: [laughing out loud] I've made SEVERAL honest efforts. We'll see.

Glynn: So are you saying you want this to continue? That is kind of how it seems.

Ginger: So, I think your Gray Rock plan is great. I can't wait to see it in action.

Phoenix: I feel like you are being defensive. I mean, we have been in this situation before. You are my girl and I don't want to see you hurting. As for me, I do not plan on allowing the same toxic shit in my life. Chris is dead to me. He will not continue to hurt me. I know you would do the same for me. I love you like a sister. Hell, you are my sister!

Glynn: I don't know, Ginger. I feel like you have been at war so long that you have become battle-hardened. Like soldiers who come back from Afghanistan, but can't adjust to civilian life, so they go back. I myself have been locked in a Narc war with

Simone for a little longer than you and DeWayne. But you have been in more wars overall. All we want is to figure out how to get you back home. Shit, at this point, it seems like going AWOL is the only way. Exit strategies are not often elaborate. It just requires aligning certain tasks to achieve the overall goal. If we get hung up on the minor specifics, or major ones, then it will blind us from what we want to accomplish. Then it just becomes something we want, not something we did. The Gray Rock advice you guys gave me scares me because it will limit my interaction with Noah. And that is heart wrenching. I understand that I have to build around it though. I cannot avoid it, but it doesn't mean I can't adapt. Those obstacles I have blocking my path, I will meet head on. Overcoming this is not going to be easy, but as long as I have a healthy support system, mental clarity, surity of self, and the willpower to GET OUT, then I will persevere.

Ginger: I'm not being defensive. I'm being redundant and it's annoying. I DO NOT HAVE A PLAN outside of getting my finances in order. I think it's ridiculous for someone to suggest that a person being narcissistically abused wants that abuse to continue. So, I ignored that nonsense and moved on. I would NEVER suggest that your repeated emasculation by Simone is something you want to continue. Fuck outta here!! I don't even know why you're coming for me. And Phoenix, you've known me close to 30 years. Your narc went to jail. Had he not, and you were still dealing with him, I wouldn't dare pass any judgments on you or think you are weak and/or dumb. I KNOW you are a mentally stable individual in a fucked up situation. I also know that you make rational decisions and you'll handle your business in due time. From years of friendship, you of all people should know that I NEVER LOSE. I either win or I learn! So, it really doesn't matter how many times or which way you form the same question, the answer remains the same. Now, if either of you would like to contribute to my household, please let me know. Otherwise, stop brow-beating me about a plan that I don't have. All of this shit is temporary!!

Phoenix: Hmmm...My intent was not to make you feel weak or dumb. I know the abuse narcs do. I also know that in time you will dissolve the relationship. But to clarify, I left Chris before he went to jail. My mother tried keeping him in my life. Like I said before, I love you and don't want to see you hurting.

Ginger: I know you do and I appreciate you. But you KNOW how I roll. In due time...But, it is wise to have a plan. I agree with that. For me, right now, I'm still figuring it all out. BUT, I DO NOT plan on a life with DeWayne.

FULL ASSESSMENT

Phoenix: Maaaaan! It is hard recovering from any toxic relationship; especially one that involves a narcissist. The shame and guilt that you feel makes you want to crawl under a rock. For some people, it could take months or even years to feel good about themselves and the world around them. It really takes a toll on your mental stability. Some people say, "The best way to get over a relationship is to get into another one."

Glynn: I would typically like to take time to myself after a relationship; not looking, not dating, and just chilling. Usually, I would just spend time with friends and try to distract myself from calling or pursuing reconciliation. But I don't know-- not everyone thinks that way. Tre once discussed with me how he didn't want to be alone. At the time, I didn't understand why. Like, for me, that was my time to reflect and contemplate. I cherished these moments with my thoughts. But what Tre told me was he preferred being around people. And that was one of the reasons he always had someone around; friend, foe, or fuckbuddy. That being alone to him was lonely.

Ginger: I needed to recuperate from my dealings with DeWayne. Then, I tried a couple of dating sites (dumb ass). Nothing worked for me. I just wasn't quite ready, I guess. I needed time. This experience with DeWayne felt like the worst experience ever. Although I can recall a few relationships that were much worse in comparison. But during those relationships, I was drunk most of the time, so I didn't feel as much. I could go to the bar and not think about those creeps. With my relationship with DeWayne, I faced life on life's terms. There was no self-medication. I'm sure that is why this relationship has lasted the longest and seemed the worst.

Phoenix: I think doing a full assessment of one's self after an abusive relationship is vital. As you stated Ginger, "I need time." We all need time to heal because what we do is create a toxic breeding ground for the next relationship. What do y'all think about not having any romantic relationships for one year after a toxic or abusive relationship?

Ginger: I agree. I took a year, but I didn't fully prepare myself for the ultimate hoover and return of the narcissist. I thought that he changed. His epiphanies and revelations seemed real, but they were just a ploy. I needed more time, to be honest, to heal and get stronger. We have to work on ourselves mentally and emotionally to overcome this.

Glynn: I have been trying to keep to myself, in a healthier way. At first I was doing it because I was depressed. Now, I just want to be away from anything that continues to cause me to feel that way. When I went on that trip, or finally escaped, the change in environment allowed me to gain some perspective on what to do next.

Phoenix: Depression, anxiety, and hypervigilance are all symptoms one may experience after being in this type of relationship. I know I was jumpy. I would even jump when my doorbell rang. There was a brief time I didn't want to leave the house, I didn't wash my ass, and I was constantly fidgeting with my fingers.

Ginger: During and after the relationship, these feelings remain for quite some time. The anxiety was the worst for me. The burning sensation in your stomach that feels like ulcers and that constant "dropping of your heart" feeling whenever their name was mentioned or you see them are all a result of the abuse.

Glynn: Yeah, the anxiety was the worst for me. That's why I HAD to take the time away from home. It was not an environment that was conducive to a healthy recovery. When I got back, I was able to think more clearly. I stopped running from my emotions and just accepted them. It led to me being able to understand who I was in the moment. But the process isn't over. The trip was more of a desperation move that just kind of worked. I didn't even get to the moment of clarity until a week or two after I got back. Which had me being flooded with everything I felt before I left. Ginger, we talked a lot during that time. And I appreciate those conversations mainly because your perspective allowed me to see things differently. Your support really helped.

Ginger: Yes, Glynn, I could see it differently because I'd been through it so many times and I knew you were too emotionally vested to think logically. Not because you're illogical, but because you were so deep in the abuse. I understood and understand the importance of having a listening ear that can relate to what you're going through. Oftentimes, when I mention narcissism to others, they look at me as if I'm talking about ghost encounters. They just can't relate. So, I get it. I get you and I get your situation.

Phoenix: I think it's important to stay away from all toxic relationships during this time. I don't care if it's family, friend, or foe! Shit, I have some people I have been friends with since grade school that are so negative and family members that are combative. Being in those types of familial relationships or friendships doesn't allow you to properly heal. As a matter of fact, it only increases the likelihood of you getting back into a toxic relationship because you are trying to maintain a homeostasis pattern that you have become accustomed to.

Ginger: Exactly! We also need to be careful not to rekindle old relationships in order to minimize our pain. I mean, nothing breaks a fall like a cushion, but we have to make sure it's not another toxic cushion that we've already crushed.

Phoenix: I totally agree! Old sex partners can be comforting, but they are in the past for a reason. I have taken my little black book out and contacted--no let me be honest--did a booty call; it left me feeling even more depressed.

Glynn: Wow. I was not expecting that. Was that when Chris was in the picture?

Phoenix: No, about a month after we separated.

Ginger: You have to protect your mental and emotional self. These toxic people leave voids in your life. Repeated exposure will definitely leave you feeling depressed. Jumping from one addiction to the next keeps you addicted.

Phoenix: Looking at the role you played in the relationship is also helpful. Whether it was good or bad. This is a step most people miss. We fail to realize it takes two to be in a relationship. So, evaluating our patterns, traits, habits, and behaviors are pivotal for change.

Ginger: Or you become the abuser.

Glynn: I see what y'all mean. When you are in recovery, you can be vulnerable to abuse from others. I was in the process of triple dipping back into one of my past relationships. But during an argument, post hook-up, she suddenly tried to tear me down. I wasn't prepared for that kind of toxic energy at the moment.

Phoenix: Yes, Glynn, we are in recovery just like someone addicted to a substance. We crave the person even though we know they are not good for us. In recovery, it is said, to stay clean you should stay away from people, places, and things that may trigger your addiction. I feel it is the same for toxic or abusive relationships. To stay away from Chris, I blocked him from my social media pages and made them private and only selected posts that do not involve me were made public.

Ginger: That is EXACTLY how I've categorized this relationship. It's addiction, plain and simple.

Glynn: That's what I hate about it. There were times I felt like an addict. I mentioned the withdrawal symptoms earlier. Sex with other women during the recovery period wasn't as fullfiling; it was like taking a placebo. Especially those times with one of my exes, Romona. She built up expectations of rekindling a relationship that wasn't feasible. And then tried to make me fit those expectations. Sheeeit, talk about projection. When we fell out, she tried to take what I shared with her about Simone and use it to make me feel worse. That was the moment that had me come to terms with rebuilding my self respect. It was one thing to get put down by the woman who had my child, but I would be damned if I was gonna let some previous pussy try to bring me down. I wasn't fully ready to stonewall Simone, but I built up resistance against others who would try to tear me down.

Phoenix: For that reason, I feel it's best to not discuss your traumatic relationships with future mates regarding past mates. It gives them permission to treat you the same way your abuser has.

Ginger: That's true. Or, if you're a narc magnet and you've found yourself in a new relationship with another narcissist, they'll use that information to love-bomb you or adjust their mode of narcissistic attack.

Glynn: It's fucked up! Sometimes that is all you wanna do; just purge all the negative emotions, treatment, and experiences you have endured. But you are right. You can't do it with just anyone. Not everyone has the empathy required to help you heal. And a lot of times they may have their own objectives. For me, I was in the relationship for longer than I needed to be. I have so much of myself that I need to relearn and reconstruct. That is a ME project. Anyone trying to come and interfere with that isn't necessarily being helpful.

Phoenix: Exactly! Having or learning self-respect is key. You have to reconcile with yourself and know that you are worthy of being treated well. You deserve to be treated with dignity and respect. As well as not tolerate being treated unfairly, being lied to, or berated. You have to consider your feelings above others. Some may call this selfish but it's not; it's self-love. It actually helps others to treat you with the respect and dignity you deserve. With that said, we must break the cycle. To do that, we must not continue to date different people with the same characteristics of a toxic person. We know the signs because we lived or are living with them. We can no longer allow ourselves to be guided by other's thoughts and opinions of us. Having self-respect creates a pathway for us to take control of our actions and behaviors without the fear of being judged or ridiculed.

Ginger: Before I understood what was happening to me, I assumed that it was ME. The common denominator in these failed relationships was Ginger. I had resigned to being a serial dater and started adopting cats. I figured that I would ultimately be alone and that was God's plan for me. Now that I understand why my relationships always fail, I actually feel better. I now know that I'm an empath. I understand that it's a blessing and a curse. I know that broken people will always try to set up shop in my life. They gravitate to my incredible aura and it says a lot about me. I also know that I have to keep a close eye on these parasitic creatures and not let them infiltrate my heart or my mind. I'm so caring that I have to remind myself to stop going overboard to help these people. They're goal is to suck all the life out of you. It's okay to have concern for others and to help if you can. I do these things at my own expense, though; mentally, emotionally, financially, spiritually, and sometimes even physically. I have to push back, learn to say no, and work on myself. But seriously, I'm on cat number 2.

Phoenix: Ginger, you have to learn to forgive yourself. You may be an empath, but you can do better and deserve better. Just because these relationships have been a pattern, you can use what you have learned and choose a different option. And, you may want to consider forgiving the people that have hurt you. I had to have a talk with little Phoenix in which I apologized to her for not being able to protect her as a child. I let her know that the past trauma she experienced was not her fault. I told her she is worthy of love and being loved. I promised to protect her above all others and she is the most important person in my life. I also forgave myself for allowing other people to hurt me and for not caring for myself first. I was in the mirror crying for hours. But, I felt much better and EMPOWERED.

Ginger: I agree. During my 12-step program, I had to forgive myself, forgive others, and ask for forgiveness from others. I took a year to work on myself. I had blamed myself for these failed relationships because of my "stinking" drinking and my "stinking" thinking. A year after I stopped, I met DeWayne and my initial relationship with him confirmed what I had suspected; my drinking is why I couldn't find a good man...until his mask slipped off. Then I blamed my no-nonsense attitude. Once I realized what was really happening to me, I stopped blaming myself and started appreciating who I am. I've forgiven myself, but I still have work to do.

Glynn: That is a part of me that I am reluctant to work on; forgiveness. I am still working on the acceptance aspect of myself. As I come to terms with what occured over the years, more becomes clear to me. I hold myself accountable for the errors I commited, the pain I caused, and the time I wasted. But where I fuck up is trying to rectify those wrongs. I can't forgive myself fully until I make things right. I won't force it though. On the flipside, I also can't forgive those who hold no remorse for the wrong that was imparted on me. This is the cycle that I am struggling to end. I have learned that I can't always make amends with others. So, instead I have settled on using it as a reminder of what not to do, what to look for, what to avoid, and why I shouldn't go backwards. It may not be the best way to move forward, but it is a placeholder until a healthier recourse is available between those I wronged and those that wronged me. As you stated Phoenix, my first concern should be that I am able to live with myself. I am the only me I will ever be.

Phoenix: I think we have to have a healthy mindset both ethically and morally. What are things we want for ourselves; are we the best version of ourselves? Does that make sense?

Ginger: Absolutely!

Glynn: Yes. I would say so. I am trying to invest more self-love into myself. That requires that I know my worth and appreciate what it is I have to offer. But what I'm offering is not exclusive to a mate, but the world. Oftentimes, that may not be apparent to people. I can't force it. All I can do is move on and move forward. I can't allow toxic people to taint my principles. Afterall, your values aren't valuable to those who don't value you.

Phoenix: Well said, Glynn! What I took from what you said is that we must find our purpose in life. Who am I and who am I with others? I am on a new path of self-discovery. Once I am healed, how do I find my place in the world? I want to use my life experiences to help others heal from their traumatic experiences. In doing so, I must evaluate the people that enter my life. Are they here to help me or hurt me or for me to help them? I know what pain from a toxic person feels like and I don't want to inflict that on anyone else. For most of my life, I have met people that shared their hurt with me. I recall a few years ago shopping at Lowe's with my best friend. There was a man a few aisles over. He looked in distress. I told my friend, "Watch, that guy is going to come over here and start talking to me about his problems." And sure enough, he did! I think I have known my purpose for a while. I just need to learn how to identify who is not healthy for me to date. You know what I mean? I know there is someone better out there for the three of us.

Glynn: Therein lies the commonality; the desire to help. We can't help those we date by fixing what is broken in them internally. It is best we use the tools we've acquired to assess what's wrong in us before we date anyone new. Doing so will allow us to know if this is a healthy person we could date or if it is an unhealthy person we can help. Being able to discern the difference between the two is akin to finding genuine love or providing serviceable advice. Getting involved with those we wish to help would muddy the process. Avoiding this is a good way of weeding out potential problems before they have a chance to take root in the heart. As empaths, our capacity to feel for others must be cautiously used. Lest it be callously abused.

Phoenix: Being an empath to toxic people is a bad habit I plan to break. Just like smoking these damn cigarettes and other bad habits! I want to be an overall healthy person. Free to make better informed decisions with a clear mind.

Glynn: I agree. I don't want to rid myself of empathy. Rather, I wish to focus it on those who most deserve it. What my past experiences have taught me is to use that ability sparingly. Before, I overestimated the capabilities of those that I shared my compassion with. Now, I shall only share who I am with those who deserve it. Once I was an open book that was easy enough to read. But I got burned. Then I tried being an enigma, wrapped in a vault of secrets, guarded by 10 story high walls, perched cliffside. I did that for my safety, but it only served to keep out potential love. Now, I will try to balance the two; being guarded but open. I will not let precedent prevent me from having a promising future. Instead, I will let hindsight be my insight and walk down a more enlightened path.

Ginger: WOW! Glynn, that's very powerful and an excellent way of approaching this. I can't help who I am and I won't allow others to turn me into a bitter bitch. I, too, will only open myself up to people who deserve me. I'm paying much more attention to who I let in and who I help. At this point, me getting burned is on me. I have to do better.

Phoenix: I was thinking. How do these relationships impact how our children's ability to form and develop relationships with their peers and how they treat us? And how do these relationships affect their self-esteem, behaviors, and mental health? I know children can feel the tension of a stressful relationship. I think it affects their sense of safety in the home. Parents are the first role model for a child and they tend to mimic their parents' behavior. Since I don't have children, have either of you noticed any impact on your child?

Ginger: Other than DeWayne, Sarah hasn't met anyone. But she does show irritation with DeWayne. She wishes that I'd find someone better. However, DeWayne treats her like royalty. She can do no wrong. He caters to her because he wants her approval. She's older and very wise, so she sees through his bullshit. William is different. He does not like his father at all. DeWayne has narcissistically abused him as well.

Glynn: [inhales deeply and exhales slowly] Ok, as you know, I am dealing with four separate adolescent minds. There is a range of behavioral traits and patterns to account for; mainly because they are ever changing. The primary focus is Noah, but his sister Leslie concerns me, too. Leslie was the precursor to Noah as I was around since she was a baby. She has adapted to her mother's behavior by essentially becoming her doll. Doted on as often as she is reprimanded for the slightest errors. I feel like Ginger most times I am with them. In that, my empathy doesn't always allow me to stay silent. I can't take custody of them though. Of all the four children I have observed, Noah is the most hyperactive and outspoken. All of Simone's sons are, to be honest. Ray is inquisitive and logical, so he recognizes Simone's BS. Kenny, however, is more verbally combative with his mom. Honestly, it is a hostile environment. And from what I see, outside of Leslie, they all kind of rebel against Simone in their own way. Sometimes I feel as though she is losing her grip on them. Her old way of verbally berating them is losing its weight. And whereas they all had to get to that point, Noah is developing under that umbrella. Ugh!! Why would you ask me such a complicated question? Damn, I ain't even got to the meat of the matter. SHIT!! You know how long winded I can be. This gonna take all damn day.

Phoenix: [laughing out loud] You could probably write a book about their interactions with Simone!

Ginger: DeWayne's other children are quite distant, except for Dewayne Jr. DeWayne didn't have a very close relationship with his two daughters. As they've gotten older, the relationships have gotten better. They didn't get the full-on narcissism like William and DeWayne Jr. I came into their lives when William was nine and DeWayne Jr. was eighteen. DeWayne Jr. was grown and had moved out before I moved to Atlanta. I couldn't do much for him, psychologically. The damage was done. Because of the abuse from his parents, DeWayne Jr. is somewhat of a recluse. He goes to work and goes home. He doesn't mingle much with the family and he stays to himself. Every once in a while, we'll have a sighting. He's clearly damaged. He hates his father, too, but continues in the relationship with him because he doesn't know anything else. Amber's abandonment of both boys added greatly to the toxicity. An absent mother and narcissistic father are both a horrible combination and extremely abusive. The boys gravitate more to DeWayne because he was present and because they don't quite understand what has happened to them over the years. Amber continues with her mental absenteeism, only being partially present in their lives; concerning herself with the simple things like a meal every now and then or an outfit for a special occasion. This is why it's so hard to leave William alone with these two psychos. Who will protect him? My empathy bleeds in pain with the mere imagination of his life if I leave him to their devices. It's a sad state of affairs for these children. I just hope I've made a difference in at least one of their lives. I'm prepared to continue to stand up for him. I love him like my own!

Phoenix: Ginger, do you think Sarah has been impacted either positively or negatively by witnessing your relationship with DeWayne? I only ask because I grew up with two toxic parents and it definitely has played a major role in decisions I have made in my life. I think because I felt rejected by my parents, I subconsciously sought the same rejection from my mate. Sometimes I don't think parents understand how their actions affect their children and that their children see more than they realize. It has a direct impact on how they form as an adult. It has taken a long time and plenty of self-evaluating to see my patterns as well as where they stem from. Not to mention seeing a professional counselor. Speaking of counseling, how do y'all feel about seeking professional help as a tool for recovering from a narcissistic relationship? I know it has been helpful for me. I have been able to focus on myself without judging myself for being in such a relationship, identify the first signs I was dating a narcissist to avoid dating another one, see how I was acting as a narcissist towards myself, and how to show empathy for myself. Shit, it was really hard to do an objective inventory of myself. My counselor also helped me to refocus on my purpose through the counseling process. I feel more in control of my life. I no longer feel like this disjointed or fractured person. I will always stay mindful of the people I allow into my space physically, mentally, emotionally, psychologically, and spiritually. But counseling is expensive! But having a peace of mind beats the alternative. [laughing] I was on a payment plan with my counselors! The cognitive restructuring my counselor helped do was vital for improving my self-esteem. It also helped that I did my own research outside of the sessions. I could keep going on and on, and on about the benefits of counseling, but I want to know what you two think about counseling for recovering from a narcissistic relationship?

Glynn: I would say it is something that is overlooked. There seems to be a stigma against receiving any kind of relationship recovery counseling. As if it is trivial or "gay". As a dude, that is typically the response to matters of that nature. Personally, I feel that it is necessary to get the tools required to repair yourself. And in order to do that, it is best to consult someone who has education, information, and insight on the matter. I mean, you can't use the 'hood tool kit of a screwdriver, hammer, and duct tape to fix everything. When I was with Simone, I thought about couple's counseling here and there. She even suggested we sit down with her pastor at some point (of course this was after I mentioned getting help, but she brought it up as an "original idea"). Working in an environment with counselors made me more aware of the true broken nature of our relationship. Overhearing some of the calls that would come in, I related to some of the people receiving help. The misconception is that these issues are common and thus can be taken care of easily. If it can't, then it's a weakness on the part of the person unable to deal with it. But that is untrue. All trauma is not created equal and everyone's trauma is not the same. Discussing these issues with a professional is how to properly identify what is actually wrong, as well as what has been consistently going wrong. In the end, it would be negligent to persist in any mentally and/or emotionally taxing state without seeking the right help. Just because it is a mental/emotional condition causing pain doesn't mean it can be ignored or mistreated.

Phoenix: Woowee, Glynn, say that shit! I think you are on the money in your assessment of recovering from a narcissistic or toxic relationship. I also agree that it can't be fixed with a "hood tool kit" as you stated. It is good to hear the perspective of a male as it is uncommon for men to discuss their abusive relationships at the hands of their female partner. I think it is empowering for men to have a space to do so. Thank you for your candor!

Glynn: Aw, shucks. Tweren't nuthin. That aside, I am still curious to hear what Ginger was going to say about how Sarah was affected by the narcissistic nature of the relationship.

Ginger: I think it had a little impact on her, but she was eleven when we moved. She didn't notice our relationship or how toxic it was until we moved in together. She was sixteen then, but the toxicity didn't show until the situation with Amber happened. I kept it hidden pretty well, but she has made comments about the relationship and knows I deserve better. She's twenty now and has made some questionable decisions in her relationships. I attribute that more to her half-abusive, half-absent father. Luckily, I wasn't toxic, so she didn't have to deal with that from both parents. Although I'm a recovering alcoholic, Sarah didn't experience much of that part either. She saw me drink, but didn't see me drunk. She'd usually be asleep when I was at the height of my drunkenness. Anyway, she's dating a pretty decent guy now, but you know I side-eye everyone because of my experiences [laughing out loud]. William is the one that I'm more concerned about because he has experienced what you've gone through, Phoenix. I feel so bad for him. He was complaining recently about why he had to be born to two "crazy" parents and asked me why she (Amber) had to leave him with DeWayne. Then he wondered if it would have been better to be with her and, staring quietly in thought, decided against that too. He's told me that he wanted counseling. I think Sarah needs it, too, because of her father. Shit, I want to go, as well. There are reasons why my empathy is over the top and why I always end up in toxic relationships. I also have an addictive personality. I need counseling so that I can learn to be more in touch with myself, understand my thinking and why things happen to me. I did an inventory during my 12-step program to get a better understanding of who I am, but I probably need more. I guess I'm so consumed with being there for my children that I am putting myself last, as per usual. I mean, I have seriously looked for counselors for William, but not myself. I figured that I could handle things better. Listening to him, I am more and more concerned about his well-being. He confides in me often. We sit in my car, in the driveway, for hours...talking about life and life's struggles. I really do feel his pain. We discussed DeWayne and I explained to him what DeWayne's issue is. He is now fully aware of his mental issues. He even looked at me one day when DeWayne was sucking his own dick and said, "Oh my God, GiGi, I get it now!" He saw it right then and sat in amazement. He told me later that what I have experienced with DeWayne, he's dealt with his whole life. Poor baby wants to get away so bad and I'm going to help him. I've been protecting him from his toxic father since he was nine. I'll do my best to help him be as successful as possible so he doesn't have to depend on DeWayne for anything.

Phoenix: Damn, G, in addition to going through all that shit with DeWayne you have to protect HIS son for the abuse too? That is fucked up! I'm just glad Sarah has not been too affected by this relationship. But, I think counseling will be good for you all; especially William.

Glynn: Yeah, I gotta admit. That is definitely some G shit.

Ginger: I totally agree, but DeWayne isn't invited. Quick side story: DeWayne told me that he went to marriage counseling with Amber. By the end of the session, the counselor was on his side. He took this as a sign that he was right. I argued him down and told him that he completely manipulated and gaslit the entire situation. I KNOW he did, without being there. So, thinking about you Glynn, wanting to go to counseling with Simone would have you looking like a psycho and validate her nonsense. But, counseling in these situations is definitely recommended.

Phoenix: I agree with you, Ginger. A narcissist can manipulate a counselor that has little or no experience with dealing with Narcissistic Personality Disorder. It is best to research counselors in your area that specializes in this area. Or, you will come off as looking like the abuser, the narc, or insane. These individuals have a knack for twisting the truth and are skilled manipulators.

But, a good mental health professional with experience in this matter can see through their narcissistic behaviors.

Glynn: I find context to be key in any given conversation. The thought that Simone could gaslight a counselor did cross my mind. Once we both talked to one of her friends about an issue and, when given context, that friend agreed with me. After which, Simone disowned that chick until she needed her for whatever. With this, I realized that any mental health professional worth her/his salt in the field would see through the manipulation; if given candid contextual conversations and the opportunity to explore the situation appropriately. That said-- NO DUDES! I don't want anyone that could get a whiff of the slightest scent of Simone's vagina and ignore the overwhelming aroma of her pungent bullshit!!

Phoenix: [laughing] Even a trained male counselor that specializes in this area could see through Simone. But, I have to go for now. It was good talking to both of you. Having someone- -in this case two someones--that understands the complexities of being in a toxic narcissistic relationship is invaluable. I want you both to know how much I appreciate you for being part of my support system. Love ya' and talk to you soon!

Glynn: Same here Phoenix. The whole thing was a journey that has impacted my life heavily. And as I have a child resulting from it, it is going to continue to be an uphill battle being his father. But with friends like you two, at least I know that it won't be something I'll be experiencing alone any more. Thank you both for your advice, your information, and just being an ear to listen. I really appreciate our conversations. I am looking forward to talking with y'all again. And I plan on being in a muuuuuuuch more positive space by then. [laughs] Later, people. Peace!

Ginger: Love you, two! Until next time…Uhhhh, well…tomorrow! [shaking my damn head with a shoulder hunch] Peace! Mic drop!

BIBLIOGRAPHY

American Psychiatric Association. (2013). *Diagnostic and statistical manual of mental disorders* (5th ed.).

 https://doi.org/10.1176/appi.books.9780890425559 6

United States Department of Justice. (2019). *17 indicted in multi-state cocaine distribution scheme conducted through the U.S. mail.*

 https://justice.gov

Big Sean (2014). I don't fuck with you. (Excerpt).

Dark Sky Paradise.

ABOUT THE AUTHORS...

Nakpangi Thomas, Ph.D., LPC, TITC-CT is a licensed professional counselor, clinical traumatologist, and adjunct professor at Southern New Hampshire University. She holds a doctoral degree in Counseling Education and Supervision from Walden University. Dr. Thomas has presented on various mental health issues from childhood adversity, human trafficking, tele-counseling, substance abuse, mindfulness, and more. She has held various leadership roles in the field of counseling and is an active member of the American Counseling Associate, Association for Humanistic Counseling, Counselors for Social Justice, and Chi Sigma Iota Honors Society. Dr. Thomas has also advocated for the counseling profession, human rights, women's rights, fair housing, as well as poverty, and criminal justice reform. In her spare time, she volunteers for local community organizations and serves as a board for several local organizations. While this is her first adventure in writing; she plans to write more novels.

Gaily Laird, B.S., MAT is a teacher of students with special needs in one of America's toughest inner cities. She holds a Bachelor's Degree in Psychology and a Master's Degree in Secondary Education. She is originally from Detroit, Michigan, but now resides in Maryland. Ms. Laird is the mother of two beautiful children; one biological daughter and a bonus son from a previous relationship. Ms. Laird is a deep-feeling empath who has encountered a number of narcissistic people and has been in numerous narcissistic relationships. From her experience, she has been able to understand the characteristics of people with Narcissistic Personality Disorder (NPD) and she considers herself a survivor of Narcissistic abuse.

Nigel Jennings is a burgeoning writer with a collection of work soon to be published. A father and introspective introvert, looking to start his first foray into writing was short stories. This being his official debut as an author, he would like to cast a light on NPD. As it is often overlooked, narcissistic abuse of men deserves an earnest voice to break stereotypes. With this genuine view from the male perspective, he hopes those who read this story come to understand how toxic emotional abuse can affect men. And people experiencing it can learn how to identify and heal from it.